Meant to Be?

Meant to Be?

*   *   *

The Wall So Strong, A Way Through Seemed a Fantasy

By Jana Vlčková and J. Daniel Lupton

ISBN: 1508818800
ISBN 13: 9781508818809

Scripture quotations taken from:
ASV, American Standard Version, Public Doman
KJV King James Version, Public Doman
ML ® The Message ® Copyright © 2002 by NavPress
NASB ® New American Standard Bible ® Copyright © 1960, 1962, 1963, 1968,
1971, 1972, 1973, 1975, 1977, 1995 by The Lockman Foundation
NKJV ® New King James Version ® Copyright © 1982 by Thomas Nelson
NLT® New Living Translation ® Copyright © 1996, 2004 by Tyndale Charitable Trust

Dedication:

This book is dedicated to our friends on multiple continents and to all our readers.

Jane and Dan

Contents:

Introduction

You've chosen a story of an unusual friendship, in spite of obstacles so numerous to make even a normal conversation seem out of reach. When the friendship begins, Dan is an American who doesn't speak Czech, while Jane is Czech, and a toddler in English, attempting to stand and walk in that language. Dan is in his sixties, Jane a teenager; Dan an English teacher, Jane a high school student; Dan a Christian believer, Jane an atheist. Our family backgrounds, national histories, town and villages, houses and holidays are dissimilar in nearly every feature.

In the first chapter, "A Strange Question," you'll encounter a wall separating two polarized worldviews. This wall appeared so impregnable, that a way through seemed a fantasy.

What made our friendship work early on were curiosity about our contrasts, and even contradictions, coupled with an open honesty, mutual respect, and integrity with facts, feelings and communication. Later the friendship grew with what might be called divine transformations. Our friendship from the beginning included Dan's wife Nancy and Jane's parents and sister, whom you'll meet. It became a friendship between two families, and in a wider arena, a friendship between two nations...Jane's Czech community of relationships and Dan's American friends in multiple states. Was this friendship meant to be?

We invite you to enjoy our story, to taste things extraordinarily wonderful, and if you find benefit in what enthused and animated us, we'll count that a bonus. Our adventure, covering a period of eight years, is conveyed in an unusual manner. We write as two witnesses telling what we observed and experienced. Each chapter is written with this dual perspective and memory. At times, in the writing process, we argued about a few incidents, regarding when and how they happened. You probably won't notice any discrepancies, but if you do, please smile and regard such as validation of realities, more authentic than any made-for-television reality show.

One more thought. While our own names are real, many of our friends have been supplied pseudonyms.

Dan and Jane

I

A Strange Question

By Jane

He came to class. His name was Dan Lupton and he was there to teach us English. This teacher came once, twice, and then every week to have English afternoon classes for student volunteers. In his very first lesson, he talked about a man crossing the Niagara Falls on a rope and then about many different things from American culture. It was all so new and special to me to have an American teaching us English. Although I did not understand every single word and sometimes found myself lost in the confusing and incomprehensible mixture of English sounds, as the teacher acted out a lot of what he was saying, I could mostly see what he was meaning. At that time, nobody would call him by his first name, though. Rather, we used the formal addressing form, Mr. Lupton, which was the only acceptable way of addressing teachers at our school.

One day we played a game, Five Against Five. I remember the students' excitement about the debate and also very comical situations which arose when somebody was trying to explain his point without knowing the proper words for it, hence they had to use gestures and pantomime.

There was also a question which sounded ridiculous to most of us, a thing we would never talk about, maybe not even think about...what would make an atheist pray? It was almost incredible to receive such a kind of question. Most of us had been raised in families with no religious background and if we would think of praying, it was only in times of fear, if anytime at all. Well, I do not know if I did answer that question in class, but I surely did not forget about it. Before the end of the lesson, Mr. Lupton gave everybody a sheet of paper with his email address and a blank box for any question we wanted to ask of him. I had noticed he was very kind and friendly. I was interested why he had actually come to our country and city so I wrote it there in the box. Soon after, the class was over and we left. There must have been about twenty of us in that group and we came from various classes of sixteen and seventeen-year-olds, from sophomore to senior classes. In groups, in pairs, or alone, we headed home that day.

I thought about that strange question a lot. My classmates had tried to comment on it in class, but not many had something to say. Somehow I felt the need to write the teacher and answer the question myself. I already had Mr. Lupton's email address; I decided to explain the matter, so that it would be clear to him. What I wrote among the first things was that in our country we did not usually talk about faith or praying. It was a very subjective and sensitive issue, which everybody should keep for himself. But there was a reason when I, a non-believer, would pray, and that would happen so many times when I was nervous about something that was part of school life...examinations. They would make even me, an atheist, pray. Funny? But it was so.

In our country, many people had a negative opinion of anything to do with religion. It might have been because of the recent four-decade era of the former regime. What was then, and still is present in people's attitude towards religion today, is if there is anything like some God, why should we care, because as they say - we can do by ourselves.

I tried to word my opinion well enough so that the teacher would understand and not ask about something like that any other time. But as I was aware of his kindness, I did not want to offend him. Feeling like talking about something positive as well, I also added my question why he had actually come and said I was glad he was visiting, because I really was. At that time, however, I still did not know that Mr. Lupton was not just a visitor, but that he was going to settle in our city. When I was writing the email, sending it out and receiving a reply from him, I would not have imagined that this would be a starting point to our lasting friendship.

Mr. Lupton replied very soon. He seemed to respect my opinion and surprisingly, he did not argue with me. He also said that he had come because he wanted to "tell people about God." I liked all he said, except this last thing. And I did not know what it actually was, so I just ignored this fact.

I would come to Mr. Lupton's every class, struggling to understand his English, and communicate with him and others in English, also. As time passed, I was becoming more confident when talking to him, as well as to other people. It was fun to be part of these classes. Not everybody kept coming as the semester proceeded, but it was even more fun to be there with those truly interested in the language. Many of my classmates gave up because they did not understand, as they were almost complete beginners in English. Who stayed in the class and was always there, though, was my friend Natasha. We shared a lot of things together. We were very good friends, visiting each other almost every day. We would sit next to each other in school, and help each other. Natasha had been my friend since we started going to high school the year before.

Very soon after our first exchanged email, Mr. Lupton invited our class to an event on Friday nights, which was called English Club. There were about twenty people and we met in a very charming environment of an old red building, the Red Library. At Club we did many different activities. There were always some games, conversation, and food. I learned a lot of new English words and was starting to pick up English faster. Each week, I understood our teacher better and better. Those attending were students from our high school and also some adults from various places in our city and outside. Mr. Lupton also introduced my friends and me to his wife, Nancy. I liked Club and I liked what they were doing and how they treated others.

By Dan

Some students giggled nervously, others fidgeted anxiously, tapping toes or twirling hair with fingers; and a few glowered angrily, not a bit happy with my questions. A mask rarely removed was uncovered with sighs and whispers and muttering that did not disguise their feelings. It wasn't my intention to anger them. This class was my responsibility, and week by week increasingly my delight. I liked them personally and loved them spiritually, and the students knew this.

I looked toward Jane. Jana Vlčková was a student in my first English Conversation Class in a Svitavy, Czech Republic high school. She introduced herself with, "My name is Jana but please call me Jane." With that phrase I understood that she knew English and could confidently speak it. Before that class session was over I knew that when students didn't understand my voice or vocabulary, I would look toward Jane for translating assistance. Jane became my student aide and soon my friend.

On this day, looking to Jane didn't help. She was a student, and today she felt very Czech. The discomfort her classmates felt was in her soul as well.

Disguising feelings is a Czech cultural feature where a raised eyebrow or only a stare, can stop a misbehaving child and cause him to return to approved conduct. With only forty-five years of freedom in the last 400 years of national or near-national existence, there developed a phlegmatic response to frustration and authority figures. Even now seventeen year old students quietly enter school classrooms and stand at attention until the teacher greets them and invites them to sit. I can't imagine any Czech student sassing or raising a voice in disrespect to a teacher. It never happened to me.

In this day's English Class, the veneer was cracking and I had a glimpse into the soul of the people. The students felt threatened by my questions and also threatened by letting me see how they felt. Such an un-Czech like moment…

This was my first year in Czech high school classrooms. Nancy and I moved to Svitavy, the Czech Republic in June of 2006. "Doors" opened for me to teach English Conversation first in the Svitavy Gymnasium, and soon in other schools. But I had no curriculum, no guidebook and no lesson plans to help me succeed. Week by week, I prepared lessons on a variety of topics to widen their world view, learn my view, and increase their confidence in verbal skills. Classes had such topics as American Schools, Yellowstone Park, Entertainment, Government, Route 66, Shopping, Directions, Housing, Foods, and holidays including Thanksgiving Day, Christmas, St Patrick's Day, Easter and Independence Day.

In the Svitavy Gymnasium [university prep high school], students elected to spend a class hour with me after normal school hours. In the USA, students will stay beyond class hours to practice for a sport; in the Czech Republic there are no sport programs in high schools or universities.

While teachers during the normal school hours have the luxury of being methodical and text bookish, my students were sacrificing other more playful interests to practice English with a native speaker. If they found this time unproductive or boring, they may quit without penalty. My classes must have some "pop and sizzle," although that idiom would mean nothing to them.

Any learning regimen can become tedious. To renew the fresh and fun elements I decided to play "Family Feud" for one class. Family Feud is a staple of Czech TV under the game show name "Five Against Five." "Family Feud" would sound rude, not cute or funny to Czechs.

To ensure student involvement all the way through, I prepared 40 questions for the Czech teens to answer a week prior to game day. From their answers, I'd choose the top five or six for the actual game. I had thirty-seven typical fun questions and three with a religious flavor.

Fun questions included,

1. What is the most important thing to have when you go camping? Tent – 41; Food/Drink – 11; Money – 4; Sleeping bag – 4; Knife – 4.

   Good answers that didn't make the final list included: Friend, Matches, Suitcase, Warm clothes, Good weather, Singing.

2. Name a Christmas tradition. Top answers were: Christmas tree, Giving gifts, Cutting an apple, Carp for Christmas Eve, Eating sweets.

So it continued…What is your favorite pizza topping? What is your favorite place for a date, favorite movie genre, favorite radio station, what sports do you watch on TV, etc.?

These were all met with pleasure, until the first religious question popped up. "Name one of the Ten Commandments." That didn't work well because they didn't know the Ten Commandments. I received only two answers from multiple class groups: Several wrote "Don't Know" and a few wrote "Don't Murder." That didn't surprise me…most American students couldn't name two or three of the biblical Ten Commandments.

Both the USA and the Czech Republic are changing in national ideals and historic memories. While some nations boast of national parks and resources, others of their universities, athletic prowess or political power, the Czech Republic often vaunts being the most atheistic nation in the world. It can also boast of renowned hockey players, of authors like Kafka, of classic and modern architecture, of Bohemian artists and musicians, of being a nation that exports more than it imports, and of being the first nation [16th century] to offer education to boys and girls, serfs and noble families. While they are aware of these causes for national pride, they also know that other nations have mottos like "In God We Trust," but Czechs are atheists. The nation is 70% atheist, and Svitavy, a former Sudeten town, is 95% atheist.

Nancy and I had only recently arrived in this nation and I wanted to know what Czech atheism looked like, so I added a second question to the "Five Against Five" list.

"What is a favorite or famous miracle of Jesus?" The students didn't like this one either, but they had some answers this time. Resurrection – 32; Turned water to wine – 11; and Walked on water – 7. With this question the whispering began in the Czech language and not in English. Jane was one of the whisperers, who avoided looking me in the eye. If someone knew a miracle, he whispered it to friends left and right, fore and aft. I didn't mind…even in this I was learning about the culture.

And these answers were more in line with what I hoped for. This atheistic nation, in many schools, offers Christian religious and Bible education, including the school I was in this day. The school's reasoning is that the Bible has been the most published, read, and influential book in Czech and European history. Since the Bible has been more popular and powerful than Shakespeare, why would they teach Shakespeare and not the Bible? The Bible is treated as both essential literature and a history source. One is not educated who doesn't know the stories of Adam and Eve, Patriarch Abraham, Prophet Moses, King David, and Jesus and the disciples. The Ten Commandments question and the Miracles of Jesus question did not provide enough responses to be of value in playing the Family Feud game the following week. What they did provide was student uneasiness, but only of the variety of not having answers to my questions. They were all in the same boat so no high schooler felt particularly stupid. They thought I was stupid for asking the question.

The question that brought the flood of disturbance was the third one: "What event would make an atheist pray?" This question brought out the sighs and giggles, the foot shuffling and the under swell of murmuring. It caused Jane to do much thinking about her life and upbringing.

I wrote the question because I wanted to test the American idiom: "There are no atheists in foxholes." The American Christian assumption is that the most ungodly relative, the one who won't go to church even at Christmas, the one who boldly asserts his atheism, will still call on God for help when bullets are flying past his head amid "the rockets' red glare, the bombs bursting in air."

To understand those I was serving, I wished to know if this idiom was true or false in the Czech Republic. The consternation in the classroom was not like that of the lack of Bible information revealed in the first two questions. "What event would make an atheist pray" probed their own hearts, inquired whether their form of atheism was a firm conviction or a casual unexamined approach to life.

When they found a detour around their anger and answered the question, I received enough good answers to use in the game the next week. The top answers to "what would make an atheist pray" were: Danger – 8; Disaster – 7; School test – 6; Injury/Illness – 5; War – 4; Nothing – 4; Desperate – 3; Death of loved one – 2; One each: Big problem, Need miracle, Need help/cheer, Driving, Dying, Kidnapped, and When facing Chuck Norris.

The Chuck Norris answer was fun. Chuck Norris is a Czech super hero and a continuing national joke. *'When Alexander Bell invented the telephone he had three missed calls from Chuck Norris. Before the Boogey Man goes to sleep, he checks his closet for Chuck Norris. Chuck Norris is the reason Waldo is hiding. Chuck Norris has already been to Mars, that's why there are no signs of life there.'*

So facing Chuck Norris would make even an atheist pray.

The total number of answers showed that many students left a blank space to this question. Only four students wrote the purest answer: "Nothing" will make an atheist pray.

That evening I received an email from Jane Vlčková. This day and this email cemented a friendship that has continued and flourished for over eight years. She wished for me to understand what happened in the classroom earlier that day. Here is her letter to me with my replies within the email.

[Jane]: Dear Mr. Lupton,

> The questionnaire, which you gave us on Wednesday, was funny and interesting. I am sorry for the mistakes I made while writing the answers to the questions. I always realize them when it is too late. I rather concentrated on my classmate's answers and not on mine. I hope you do not mind the mistakes in grammar. And also that it was written with a pencil. I thought about you and your belief. You can think that some Czechs including me consider God to be somebody who may be there but is not so important, who is not a part of our life.

[Dan]: Dear Jane,

> Actually, I think most Czechs consider God to be a myth who is not there. But I also believe God has given each of us an intuitive knowledge that he is there and that he is good and kind and loving. This nation has become what V. Havel feared, and T. Masaryk before him, something that has never been in the history of the world to now - a nation of atheists. Yet at one time the Czech people knew God and liberty and education and family life better than any people on earth.

[Jane]:

> Some students might have been a bit confused when seeing the questions regarding God. Maybe because we do not know much

about him. That is the difference between American students and the Czech ones. When I attended the basic school, a priest or a man who worked in a church came and offered us to attend the church and learn something about God. At that time just four children lifted up their hands. Other children did not want. That might have been because the belief was not in their family (they were not religious). In my family except for grandpa and granny who are, but who have likely stopped believing as I have never seen them praying, nobody believes in God. When I was growing up I was living in the conviction that if somebody is religious they are old-fashioned.

[Dan]:

I notice the joy difference in older people -- people my age. I think young, but the mirror tells the truth. Those who are my age and know God as Father and Jesus as Savior live with a lifetime accumulated joy and the hope that everything will get better. When they leave this world their lives step up to a higher joy in heaven. Sometimes I try to imagine being a 60+ unbeliever with nothing exciting to look forward to. Does that make sense? The Czech believers in the Litomyšl church are full of joy. Sunday morning is a weekly family reunion. I know Czechs with faith all over this land and I feel they are the ones who really enjoy life and live with inner peace.

[Jane]:

Mr. Lupton, also know that when the boys and I was laughing last lesson while thinking what should make an atheist pray or what is Ten Commandments (now we know:-)) or when I showed to my friend what is to pray we did not want to affront anyone. I am an atheist. I have not found so far a belief which I would like. Maybe sometimes I will find it and maybe not. I think that if somebody is religious or not is not so important. What is important is to behave and think well. This letter might have exhausted you so I will finish soon.:-)

[Dan]:

I thank you for the gift of trust to write to me the truth of what you feel. You would not tell this to a stranger. Something in you said you must write this to me and that I will still care for you - I wouldn't reject you. It is so.

[Jane]:

This week was very busy. Fortunately the weekend is coming. I am going to read a book now. Nobody is at home so there is peace and quiet here. Have a nice time, Jane

[Dan]:

I wish real peace for you all the time, Your teacher friend, Dan

II
Who Meant It To Be?

By Jane

A year before Mr. Lupton arrived, I was fifteen, entering high school in September, and thinking about everything else but studies. This school time was also everything except what I was hoping for. Growing up, I saw American television sitcoms, about teenagers and young adults. They kept showing young people enjoying themselves, partying, having fun, and a good time with their friends while they were in high school. And that image appealed so much to me. What frustration it was when I finally came there and encountered only studies, studies, and nothing but studies, as the only priority of high school time and maybe the only interest of my classmates.

From the very beginning, we were called a very hard-working and unique class of students. There were classmates who studied every day to give the right answers when the teacher asked them. They all seemed to be so happy about their new school, so committed.

I was used to some classmates being disrespectful to teachers when I was in middle school, although it was not done so much openly, as they kept their criticism mostly for themselves. Anyway, I really found no pleasure at all in learning, except for some subjects I had always enjoyed. While most of the classmates were excited about being in high school, I was unhappy and miserable.

Since our school desks were for two people, I sat next to a friend I had met in a ballet course two years before. Her name was Lydia, and she was one of the brightest students in our class. Lydia was also one of the Christian believers we had in our class. We must have had about four believers out of thirty students. They received a reputation of being hard workers immediately after school started, and the teachers really liked them. These classmates were also the real opposite of the young people in the TV series I admired and wanted to follow.

However, what luck it was to me when I saw that in our class, I could find somebody seeking the same as me – timeout from schoolwork and enjoyment of some real life. It was Natasha who introduced us. And it was awesome that the three of us lived in the same neighborhood where we could visit each other almost every day. Sometimes we did homework together; other times we just talked. My new friend socialized exactly with the kind of people I felt attracted to. Not with the uninteresting students from my class, but teenagers who were seeking what an adults' real life was about. Of course, we could not spend much time over textbooks... such young people had to step out and take their chances in life.

I was convinced that the way I had been trying to excel when I was in middle school was only a waste of time. I used to be the number one student until I was fourteen, when I could no longer bear my classmates' mockery because of good grades; I did not want to stand out in the crowd anymore. The teachers' saying I had the best test was suddenly not gratifying, but making my situation even worse. I was embarrassed for receiving good grades. I wanted to be average, to be like the majority, be accepted by my peers, and go with the stream. We were hardly ever encouraged to be the best. No words were spoken about where we were academically and what we could achieve.

Unhappiness enveloped me a lot in those days. I was tired of being teased by well-known bullies from our class, whom teachers could mostly do nothing about. With all of this peer pressure, and with a desire for something different, a desire for beauty, a desire for good friends and acceptance, I wanted change.

I was also often sick with a reoccurring infection with my tonsils. I first had problems at the age of nine. Sometimes it was seemingly better; other times I had problems every day. It seemed like I had tonsillitis all the time; the abscesses were chronic. Consulting specialists and taking various medications gave no long term results. I was tired of being sick a lot, as well as other things, so I said goodbye to an art course I had been taking for seven years.

At that time, still in middle school, I started a modern dance course, based on ballet. Our teacher was a very talented lady who everyone admired. I was completely enchanted by the dance. The first lessons were hard, but I kept trying. Sometimes it was quite discouraging because I couldn't keep up with the other girls. I liked to dance in an empty hall all by myself when there was no one else there, just music, dance and me. Both dancing and exercise had served me well during this period and brought more joy into my life. I even fantasized that after middle school I would go to a conservatory to dance ballet and perform in beautiful concert halls, wearing all the fancy outfits of ballet dancers. We had recitals and it was all very inspiring to me. I thought I was doing a good job until I received bad grades on my certificate at the end of the semester, whereas, my classmates got mostly good marks. I remember I was devastated, as I thought the scores were only a formality and expected everybody to get only good grades.

Even though I only took modern dance for two years, the girls in the course who were my age had known each other for a long time. I tried to be friendly to them, although I knew some of them liked to tease others back at their school. Lydia was the only one who was truly my friend. One day we heard the girls talking about their boyfriends. Although we were only fourteen and fifteen, they were rather experienced in relationships with boys. Some of them prided themselves on having one boyfriend after another. We also heard the girls talking about boys when we were performing at a concert in a faraway city. This trip was filled with their chatting about beauty, chasing after boys, buying make-up and perfumes. Lydia confided in me later that she heard one girl saying to another, that she wanted to go to bed with her boyfriend. After that trip, Lydia and I promised to each other, we would never do that unless we were married. But could we, or would we, keep that promise?

This was the last year of middle school and I felt the peer pressure from my classmates was increasing. What is more, everybody around me seemed to be changing; they were no longer children. We were all growing up and excited about different things than before. I stopped understanding my classmates. They were mostly interested in relationships, dating, gossip and going to discos. Some of them had started smoking. Some came to school dirty and smelled of cigarette smoke. Very often, under their desks they read magazines that were like manuals of flirting.

That year, my good friend, Anna, with whom I had been a friend for seven years, and I drifted apart. She started liking another friend of ours better than me and spent more time talking to her about a boy Anna liked. Not wanting to lose our friendship, I didn't want to leave the two girls alone. On one occasion, we were walking back from lunch and Anna was supposed to have a meeting with the friend. I wanted to be present. After they exchanged worried looks and started laughing, I understood it was time for me to go. I was determined not to be her friend and not talk with her anymore. We would never do mean things to each other during this time. It was just as if the other had stopped existing; it was shocking to everybody and teachers were worried because this divided our class into two camps. Our parents were wondering what happened. Yes...this was the sad end of our friendship.

But in all of this, I still had my beloved dancing and music and some friends like Ludek and Marek. Ludek would call me "Prossefor" instead of "Professor" in our Physics classes. We had a lot of fun together. Ludek and Marek liked to talk about occultism and spirits. They were attracted by what was secret, mysterious and frightening. And I liked to listen to their scary stories. We planned to go and induce spirits together in an old school on the edge of our city, but we never got to do it. I tried it with my neighbor once and it got scary, so we stopped. Ludek and I stayed friends even after each of us went to a different high school.

Toward the end of our last year in middle school, everybody took it easy; nobody studied, to the teachers' concern and sometimes irritation. I was no longer active in class and did not excel in anything. Was I trying to be like my classmates...or trying to be myself?

My first middle school disco dance was on the last day of April, which is an old Czech tradition, called "Burning of Witches." I went there with other friends; I don't remember if I had asked my parents for approval. But if I did, I surely did not return by the promised time. I knew a cute boy from our class would be there. He had actually even invited me there. However, when we got there, he only said, 'hi' and danced the rest of the night with another girl. I danced with another boy and when I went to school next day, there were rumors that we were kissing and it was a big issue.

That night while I was at the disco, there was a woman driving around desperately looking for her child. That child had just stopped dancing with a boy and answered a phone call. It was my mom. Her voice sounded very worried and even angry. She was very disappointed at me for having gone to the disco and not coming home. I did not dare talk to her about it. I said I was sorry I had caused her to look for me and that I was fine... but was I? I had been admitted to the best high school in our area. I had also won a competition for the city's logo. I had just received a kiss from a boy and had friends I could talk to about my problems. But I was tired of the way some people treated me, and tired of my tonsillitis that kept reoccurring and which I could not do anything about.

Struggling with ever changing teen-age emotions, I felt like I was living a separate life from my dad, mom and sister. I loved them, but I wanted something else from life and I knew what it was...to forget about myself, the misery of my illness, and many people around me. I wanted to enjoy myself and try something new. I wanted to be an adult even though I did not know how to do it. It was a struggle to find myself. I did not want my family to be hurt. I wondered if my parents were disappointed in me. I wanted all the best for them, but I did not always want to be with them. I thought they did not understand my needs and my desires. I was afraid of being judged again because so many times people labeled me. Sometimes I was treated badly by others, and I did not have any intention to treat those people kindly either. There were some good things in my life then, but more things that were painful and seemingly never-ending.

During summer vacation before high school, I went to another even bigger disco in a nearby village. The boy from the Burning of Witches disco was there, but we only danced. He had the reputation of being one of the skirt chasers in our town. I thought it was cool to be one of the girls who such boys had relationships with. Being a girlfriend to someone like that means being popular - or not? I danced with several boys, but we never did anything but dance. I enjoyed the music. In the light of the reflectors and with this music, I could concentrate on dancing only and forget about the world around.

It was said there were drugs at the disco, but I never saw anything like that. I mostly danced and had a good time listening to the music. I did not even drink much alcohol. The high prices deterred me. I saw the staff there as well. These poor people were from nearby villages, maybe even from the village where our family's cottage was. They stood by the entrance, or served fries with ketchup to young people like us who wanted to enjoy ourselves. I felt sorry for them and always tried not to look too disrespectful of them. In my mind, people from villages were always nicer, more sensitive, less cruel, and less indulged.

The women there who did the cooking had the kind-hearted look of such people. I could hardly look at them in their eyes, maybe because I did not want them to think I was one of those crazy young people who did bad stuff, because I actually did not. The person who took us there at night and back in the wee hours of the morning was an elderly man and just happened to be our bus driver. He drove for a party of wild, crazy, desperate, depressed, young people; maybe addicts, maybe in love, ready to do things that would not help them in any way.

When I started high school, Natasha and I spent a lot of time together. She was one of the few friends I had. Lydia had learned about me going to discos and our relationship became cold. Natasha and I could talk about many things in our lives. I was happy to have such a good friend. Once when we were talking about some problems, we tried taking out one angel card from a package. These were cards with beautiful drawings of angels and fairies and there was something written below, usually encouraging things that we should not give up, but keep struggling. I liked those cards and we took them as inspiration for life.

One day, my friend said to me her mom could tell me the future using her tarot cards. I did not have any idea of what I should do in the future and was sometimes quite desperate about it. Sometimes I also had very high expectations of myself and was full of excitement about what was going to happen - it was a desire for something greater which would exceed my expectations. So I agreed, and on that day I became attracted to the cards, and looked for the truth in them for many months that followed. When I was in distress I would ask the cards.

Natasha and I enjoyed spending time with the friend who liked to stay with popular people. In the meanwhile we had become best friends. We would talk and walk home from school and do homework together. We also had parties at her house. Their house was splendid. It was large, modern, and beautiful with lots of rooms. It was this friend who introduced me to a boy who became my first boyfriend. He was a good-looking boy who I actually never got to know well, though. We kept seeing each other outside, even though it was winter. I know it was not right, but I did not want the relationship to become too personal by inviting him over to our house. We did not talk much. It was mostly about staying together physically, not about words. We would spend hours just sitting in embrace. He was physically there, I was physically there, but sometimes I was also somewhere completely different in my thoughts. I liked this boy and I gave him a lot, but I never gave him what he gave me and that was love.

Sometimes I would get hopeless about our relationship that seemed to make no sense, and kept crying because I felt sorry for him, and even my-self. But still I believed our relationship should stay just like that - at the physical level, but no feelings involved because you do not need feelings in such a relationship. I was staying with him only because of our mutual physical attraction and I hoped he felt the same although he did not, which I learned later. I knew he might have had some girls before me. He mentioned his ex-girlfriend sometimes, but I did not mind. After all, we were together just to try something new, to experiment, maybe to experi-ence someone's closeness, but in any case to stay together just for some time, and then split up. In a world where long-term relationships were not 'in' among young people I was socializing with, and virginity was just a person's shame, what should we do? Later I saw the relationship was not giving me what I was hoping for – maybe some more joy and fulfillment. Maybe more hope? Although we were going out together for another month afterwards, I knew it was over. Saying goodbye broke his heart. And mine? Don't ask about my heart...I myself did not know. I did not even want to know. I still struggled with sadness and feelings of confusion about my own life and wanted only to forget.

Soon after our relationship ended, I received a message from an old classmate of mine and was in for a new relationship. I remember getting the message when I was just reading *Red and Black* by Stendhal. Dating this new boyfriend was very similar to my previous one, with just one dif-ference. This time neither of us really loved the other one. Whereas the first relationship lasted several months, I got tired and hopeless about this one after a few weeks and the relationship ended.

I had wanted to have many relationships. Some people I knew changed their partners one after another, so was it so bad? I wanted the kind of relationship adults had, but I was not willing to invest my feelings. So far, relationships with boys did not satisfy what I was looking for; I got tired of my choices and searching for happiness. Now I really felt I needed change. A change I would not find in relationships with boys. A change that I thought would come from a different lifestyle.

In the meanwhile, the chronic tonsillitis had worsened again and I experienced a lot of misery. No medications helped. After confiding in my friend's mom about the illness, she offered to take me to a healer who came to our city every month. He was an African man who was said to be a seer and have healing powers. I was shaking when I came to him and told him. He was rather scary. He listened and said I did not have to be so unhappy. He gave me some tea and tablets and I kept taking the medicine for more than one year. It did not bring any change, though. Some people also sent me 'energy' as they called it. I did not know what it actually meant, but at least I had their support.

My grades in high school were poor and it was almost the end of the first term. I started working hard when our Czech teacher began to talk about the Renaissance period in Literature. The period of Renaissance and Humanism brought a spiritual revival. It was something new after the long grey period of Middle Ages marked by many wars, conflicts, famine, poverty, building of stone churches, monasteries and convents, and people looking forward to leaving this world so that they could enjoy life in Heaven, rather than life on Earth. It was also during our lessons about the literature of that period of history, that nothing very pleasing was going on in my life. Maybe even that is why the Middle Ages seemed to me to be so sad, depressive, and dark, but there was this Renaissance and suddenly people (alright, especially men at that time) were encouraged to live a happy life and get an education. They wanted to make the most of their lives while they were here. It was not a spiritual awakening in the Christian sense; rather, it talked about a harmonically developed man as the center of all happening. A man educated, working on his talents and glad in what he was doing. This new chapter encouraged me to study and read. I became more interested in school. I realized the choices I had been making before led to self-destruction. The Renaissance period seemed to come and reflect itself even in my own life. Now I tried to find joy in my school subjects, and working for school all the time helped me forget.

When Mr. Lupton came, I was again one of the best students in my class, still experiencing Renaissance in my life, in my decision to live differently and work hard. School motivated me and I again found pleasure in learning new things. Our teachers kept us busy all the time. I had started to think about what I was learning and to enjoy my study. I started appreciating solitude. And I saw that the "boring" students were actually very nice and friendly, and that I could learn from them. I realized I was no longer interested in having fun with others at discos and balls. Very often I sought the quietness of my room where I could be alone with my books. I also liked to imagine what my life would be like in the future. I sometimes still had feelings of sadness and hopelessness of living, but there was almost no time for depression as I tried to make myself quite busy with school.

It was in May of my sophomore year of high school, when our English class received an invitation from Mr. Lupton for a summer camp in the mountains. This camp sounded nice. It was an English Camp with American teachers, English learning, and activities. Maybe just one thing did not sound too attractive to me and that was the fact that a church organized this Camp. However, I thought about the invitation several times and decided in the end that it was a unique opportunity for me to improve my English. English was the reason why I finally said yes. Even though I was uncomfortable about the church thing, my friend, Natasha was going to camp with me, also.

Before we left for English Camp in July, I was careful to tell Mr. Lupton in a brief email that I was going there only because of the language, that I was a definite atheist, and that it would stay that way no matter what, and that I hoped he understood.

By Dan

"It was meant to be." I hear it often, occasionally following something positive that has happened, but more often in resignation. "I didn't get the job...it was meant to be." People with faith say it, and also skeptics and atheists. And I wonder, if no God or god is there with his mind, will and power, who intended this to happen?

Jane Vlčková and I met in October of 2006. Was the convergence of our paths an accident, or something more? My passion for the Czech people, however, was birthed not in 2006, but decades earlier in 1968.

In the late 60's, I was the morning announcer for Radio station WMPC in the thumb of Michigan. One of my responsibilities was to receive the teletype news, select items for broadcast and read the news on the hour. This was the era of Prague Spring...my heart felt deeply the desire of the Czechoslovakians to live free of their Russian controllers and the one party system. Russia resented the attempt for freedom and sent in its army. Tanks rolled up Wenceslaus Square, blasting away at the Prague National Museum, which the Russian Army erroneously thought was the parliament building. Alexander Dubcek, the leader of the hope for a more independent nation, was forcibly taken to Moscow for a week and then returned to give a speech to the nation, a speech of capitulation to and compliance with Russian rule. Even now I emote as I recall Dubcek's faltering words, his breakdown and long tearful silences as he ended the hope and ushered in twenty years of despair.

That nation and its disappointment was important to me, but I never imagined that Nancy and I would one day live there and become Jane's friend. Even in 1968, my heart was being prepared...as in *meant to be.*

My focus on Czech [Czechoslovakia then] welfare was renewed in an era parenthetically marked by two speeches. The first was President Reagan in Berlin challenging, *"Mr. Gorbachev, open this gate! Mr. Gorbachev, tear down this wall!"*

Following that speech, the Soviet nation states found themselves caught between the proverbial "rock and a hard place." The rock was the rising will of the people to be free and the hard place was unsustainable national debts. The dominos began to fall as nation after nation overturned communism for western democracy.

The second speech was the new Czech President Vaclav Havel's New Year's Address to the Nation, 1990, which concluded with, "People, your government has returned to you!"

How thrilled I was with these events. I didn't rush over to meet Jane, who was born at this time, but the one *who meant it to be,* was arranging our coming friendship.

In Wisconsin, the Pastor of Kenosha Bible Church was Wayne Matejka who had relatives in Svitavy, the home town of famed Oscar Schindler of "Schindler's List," who, in a factory nearby, rescued 1,200 Jewish lives. After the Velvet Revolution [Nov/Dec, 1989] overthrew communist authority, Pastor Matejka flew to Czechoslovakia to look for cousins, aunts and uncles he had never before been able to meet. In Svitavy, his host was a math and English teacher in the Svitavy Gymnasium. I would later teach in that high school and meet that teacher...and meet Jane Vlčková.

A couple of years after Pastor Matejka's initial trip, the Kenosha church began an outreach service of providing summer English Camps. Until January of 1990, Russian was the required foreign language in schools and few had opportunity to learn English, which was emerging as the world's language of business and education. English Camps give students the opportunity to meet, listen to, and talk with native English speakers. The church provided a wonderful service, meeting a felt need of Czech students. As Christian leaders, they also told their personal stories of school and romance and struggles, and included how faith and God and Jesus were interactive in their lives.

In 2000, I became Senior Pastor of this congregation upon Wayne Matejka's retirement. Soon after Elder Chuck Heller explained to me, "each summer our church sends a team of teachers to the Czech Republic to serve in an English Camp. Pastor Dan, you don't need to make a commitment to be involved in this, but the elders wish you to go one time. As our leader you should be informed on what we do in the Czech Republic."

Nancy and I soon were preparing English lessons with the adrenaline pumping in our veins. We were headed to this nation I had cared for since the failed "Prague Spring" of 1968. But we didn't speak Czech...none of the team did. Would we feel strange, or worse, experience culture shock? Would we enjoy our time there or count the hours until we would return to the USA?

You're ahead of me if you anticipated me to say we had a wonderful two weeks. We made friends of campers and Czech adult leaders. The only comfort in saying goodbye was the promise that we'd return the next summer, which we did, and the next summer. I began to receive invitations to speak in Czech churches and felt comfortable everywhere...it was a delicious adventure. One year, I went to the Czech Republic twice to attend weddings of two friends. In 2005, I also went in January on a vision trip. The purpose was to explore ways to expand our service to Czech students and churches.

But the summer of 2005 was to be my first to miss an English Camp. It felt strange to not prepare English lessons but I gave up my team place for another. With 72 hours until departure for the English Camp, one of the Kenosha families had a medical emergency, and that would leave the team one short...one too few teachers. Who would fill the vacancy?

It needed to be someone with a Passport, and someone with enough experience to step in on three days' notice. A ticket was purchased and I was on my way, while Nancy went to China to serve in an English Camp on the Chinese Mongolian border.

Returning home, we both knew that things were changing within the church, within our hearts and within the Czech Republic. Pastor Daniel Smetana of the Litomyšl Církev bratrská [Czech Brethren] met with his elders and prayed for Svitavy. Soon they wrote to us asking if we'd consider a move to Svitavy. They had successfully planted churches in three others cities but were struggling in Svitavy. I remember the email included, "SOS, Svitavy calls." That call reached our souls, and after some months of preparation, Nancy and I moved to Svitavy in June of 2006. The Jane Vlčková we must meet was getting closer, as our Shepherd steered our paths toward convergence.

In Svitavy, we met the mayor, the headmaster of the Gymnasium [high school], and had a Core Team to work with in planting a church. This team is still intact and has grown, "friends for life," as junior highers expect.

The Gymnasium recruited students for me. Time with native English speaker Dan Lupton is extracurricular so they couldn't compel students, but I received a double roster of eager students.

Jane was present on day one...convergence had occurred. But at that time we had no way to suspect the exciting life adventure we were beginning. Each week, Jane and Natasha were in their places, the first to arrive and to sit by the window, or maybe it was the warmth of the radiator they sought. My memories of this first year are divine, blessed, rich in every way. We had classroom debates, parties, and double Christmas classes - one a party, and one what Christmas was all about to me. We sang "*Silent Night*" with a candle, and students did not wish to leave the room...they knew something special was happening among us. It is my practice to daily look for God to be active in my life. I sense His presence when he helps me serve someone, provides some special need, encourages me or uses me to encourage someone else. In this party we sensed his presence.

The high school class agreed to go to Terezin, a WWII Jewish Internment Camp an hour from Prague. Hebrew families had been rounded up like cattle and sent to the Terezin corral before being shipped to the Auschwitz slaughterhouse. Terezin is now a Czech national memorial. Students travel there to learn from the past and permit the holocaust to seep into their memories, preventing a repetition. Jane and Natasha became my guides, interpreting all that was said, making sure I was at the meal times, and ushering me from the museum to the next tour to a workshop. All my needs were cared for in such a kind way. The God *who meant it to be*, who brought about our convergence, had now arranged a special friendship.

Another feature in our growing friendship was "English Club." Two Friday evenings per month we used the Svitavy Red Library building for this club. It was a time to know students out of the classroom, in an environment of friendship and games. Jane became the anchor of the club, inviting friends and accepting game or music assignments. Through this club, I soon met her sister, Eva, with her dad and mom. Our two families soon enjoyed times together at school events and in each other's homes.

Through this first year Nancy and I grew to appreciate Jane, her sweet temperament, her willingness to help, her fearlessness in befriending us foreigners. Her serving spirit evident in our early friendship was a bud to grow into a fruit 100 fold. Many in Svitavy know my hobby is driving people home after an event. Like a horse heading for the stable, my car knew the way to Jane and Eva's house.

In the spring of 2007, I invited high school and university students to register for English Camp. We posted advertising posters in schools and all over town. Jane and Natasha were the first to register for English Camp. Worried that our camp capacity of 50 would quickly fill, they were the first two to sign up. I never told them, but they weren't being silly. We did fill those 50 beds, and all these campers were filled with English growth, new friends, and some encountered God for the first time. *He meant it to be.*

III

Flee and Hide

By Jane

On the very day of our departure, Mr. Lupton and Nancy came for Natasha and me and together we traveled to the mountains. We liked the beginning of English Camp a lot. There were Americans whom we could talk with and there were about fifty of us. Mr. Lupton was always nearby, one of the few people I knew, which made me feel more confident. All was fine.

In the first Bible story lesson though, a girl ran out of the classroom in tears. She wanted to reach her room that was opposite the classroom but, oh no, there was a class inside. Finally, she managed to get to the bathroom to wash her face. When she left the bathroom, there was another girl from the staff waiting to ask her what had happened. She was barely able to speak. What was the thing that made her cry?

"If you had one question, what would you ask God about?" teacher Dewey asked his class in the first Bible lesson. There were about ten campers and nobody spoke a word. People were sitting with their heads bowed down, thinking. Pin drop silence. Everybody was wondering what he or she would ask God about. The silence seemed to have no end. The teacher suddenly looked out the skylight and said: "God is so powerful." And his eyes filled with tears.

That was more than I could handle. When I saw the teacher crying, I could not help crying either. I was crying because the question was impossible, and what resulted was only hopelessness. How can he be asking us what we would ask God about if there is no God? We cannot ask him about anything because he simply does not exist. And we are lost. I remembered my family. My parents and sister were having a vacation at the seaside and I had not gone with them, just to be at Camp. I missed them and I thought to myself, I should have gone with them and not come here.

I was crying because I felt pressure on me. I was crying because somehow I was sorry for those people blindly believing in somebody who does not even exist. And I was angry with myself because I did not want to be crying. When the teacher said, "God is so powerful," it was as if my whole life passed before my eyes. I did not even fully understand my tears and I did not understand why I was suddenly feeling guilty. I was shocked to feel like crying and when I did cry I didn't want other people to see me. That is why I had to quickly leave the classroom.

Later I told the staff person who had been waiting to ask what had happened, that I was an unbeliever and that I did not want to be pushed into anything. But did the teacher push me? At that moment, I was even determined to go home. She said, "I felt the same, but now I think differently," and she added that she was now a believer. She also apologized for the teacher's behavior and later that day even the teacher himself wrote me a letter in which he excused himself for talking so much about God. But was it his fault that I was so touched by it?

I remember that on that night I was talking to Natasha who was in the same class. It was an angry talk about the way Christians force people, who don't believe, into believing. I must have hurt the heart of a girl from a Christian family, who had not yet become a Christian, and who shared the room with us and heard all I said. At one moment during our talk, I was just speaking about the stupidity of the idea that God could exist when I actually could not talk any more. It came to mind...but what if he exists. I did not pay too much attention to it, but that thought remained with me...but *what if* he exists?

Mr. Lupton looked concerned, but did not question me about what had occurred. He was just there, always ready to talk and listen. I knew. During Camp, I became friends with our teacher, Dewey, and his wife, Connie, their son, all my classmates and other campers and staff. Some of the classmates were people I have remembered so far - a man in his thirties who later turned out to be a Buddhist and a quiet boy from a believing family, who I was sure was a believer, although he was not, as I later found out.

One of the camp days was my birthday and just imagine – I received a cute doughnut with a tiny candle in it with everybody singing me the "Happy Birthday" song. Mr. Lupton and Nancy then gave me a beautiful cup showing the man of the mountains, called Krakonoš in Czech folklore. It was all so special and made me feel very welcome.

Actually, the Christians who were at Camp were very friendly. I was first suspicious why the people were so nice and whether their motives were pure. Before I came to Camp I knew some Catholics and only a few Protestants from my grandpa's side. All I knew about Catholics was that they had beautiful churches where I sometimes liked to peek to see the inside, and sense the silence. The churches had something special about them; they were somehow peaceful. I knew there were many statues, they used sacred water, and their priests could not marry. Of course, there were other things, which were widely known – like their worship of the Virgin Mary and saints. Protestants were even more distant to me. But as I had been to my grandpa's relative's funeral in a Protestant church when I was a child, I knew their churches were not decorated. I really did not know anything else. I was a little bit worried because for some reason I believed Protestants were adherents to various sects. I personally thought it was rather foolish to believe, but knew nothing else about Christianity.

At Camp, there were quite a few Christians, but those, to my surprise, seemed to be normal people. I saw that they could have fun and laugh like unbelievers. In our class there was a Czech lady, Irena, who was very nice and helpful to all of us. After Dewey announced that the Bible was a historical book in the second Bible lesson, in every lesson that followed we would read some stories about Jesus. Dewey helped with English vocabulary and Irena then explained the meaning of it if we still did not understand Dewey's explanations. The stories seemed to be very simple at first sight, yet very deep. It was pretty amazing what Jesus did and how he helped people. He healed them and refused nobody. All that was said about him was new to me. I quite liked the stories about him and his disciples.

Every evening we had a program with songs and dancing, which I enjoyed, but was also difficult for me at first, because we were singing many songs about God. Somehow I got used to it, though, and later it was fun to dance and sing with others. There was also a special part in the evening programs when one American and one Czech believer talked about how they had come to know God. Those stories sounded so incredible but also so real. Some testimonies, as they called them, were more serious and some were funny. I started seeing that there was something special about those people - they possessed something that I did not have.

We also had a few speakers who came to the evening program from outside. One was an older man with his wife, who talked about having to go to jail during the time of the past regime in our country, just because they were believers. They were nice people who shared a lot about their life with us. Almost at the end of Camp a pastor came and played a short movie for us. The name of it was *The Bridge*. There was a girl who was a drug addict, giving herself a shot in the restroom on the train. At a nearby train station, a bridge needed to be let down for the train that was approaching, to go over it. The man who was responsible for raising and lowering the bridge had his son there with him. The son was playing around and finally he hid in the place where the bridge was supposed to be laid. The train was coming fast and the father realized the boy was hiding there. Not letting the bridge down would mean the entire train ending up at the bottom of the gorge, causing everybody to die. Although he loved his son so much, he let the bridge down to save the lives of the people on the train. It broke his heart, but his son's death enabled people to survive. Surprisingly, only the drug addict noticed the man's desperate expression when the train passed through the bridge. The man noticed her, too. A few years later, the man saw the girl at another train station all changed and beautiful with her little son running around her happily. His son's death was not useless...

I did not fully understand the movie when I watched it that first time. It was very tragic to me. The pastor explained to us that similarly to the story in the movie, God sent his Son, Jesus, to die for us so that we could live. And that Jesus was the bridge over the gorge of sin that separates us from God.

The pastor also suggested that those who wanted to talk to him about the movie or pray with him, or even give their lives to Christ should see him afterwards. I was sure moved by the movie, but did not feel it was time for me to have a deep talk with somebody I hardly knew.

The movie left me a little sad and thinking. But that was nothing new below the sun. I had been used to depressive images from school subjects like literature and history. Almost all the works of art, which were praised by literary scientists, are full of the same, told just in a different way – love, but mostly unhappy love – the kind of love which has no chance to succeed in the world because there are so many obstacles; or platonic love so very common in novels, unhappiness, suffering, violence, depression, murder, infidelity, passion, lust, despair, scandal, addictions, cruelty, hopeless existence, an individual lost and feeling no way to escape from this world. Of course, there are books written that contain more pleasing thoughts like happiness, family life, childhood, faithfulness, virtues, but those do not seem to be so highly appreciated. I was used to reading only about hopeless things in books, and strangely, I kind of liked it.

But while English Camp had some serious moments, it was truly, very enjoyable and full of enthusiasm, friendships, learning, and exciting memories. It was so enjoyable, that at the end of Camp, I did not want to leave. I had experienced something that week, I had never experienced before.

All the people were so nice and friendly. I felt accepted.

Although I tried to resist at first during Camp, something broke in me and I started seeing...

that God...

existed.

I know...I am saying it so all of a sudden. But this process started at the beginning of Camp. Somehow I could not explain that, but there was such peace among the people...

I saw God really was there...

And I was sure about it.

Camp was over so soon. I had promised to my new friends, I would come to the English Camp church service on Sunday. It was Saturday and Mr. Lupton drove me home. My family was still at the seaside so I was home alone.

By Dan

This was my first English Camp for the Svitavy District. It will be difficult for you to feel the tug of war in my heart between the excitement and the anxiety as that day approached in the summer of 2007.

Charles Dickens expressed such tension this way, "It was the best of times, it was the worst of times, it was the age of wisdom, it was the age of foolishness, it was the epoch of belief, it was the epoch of incredulity, it was the season of Light, it was the season of Darkness, it was the spring of hope, it was the winter of despair...we were all going direct to Heaven, we were all going direct the other way" [*A Tale of Two Cities*, 1859].

Well, that's a bit overdramatic, but I knew this week would be either the year's highlight or a disappointment for me, and that among the campers there would be struggles between wisdom and foolishness, belief and skepticism. I also knew that teens and young adults were not immune to despair and a search for hope; and some were wondering if Heaven could be real or if, "life was only a candle flame that burns for a short while and then is extinguished. When the smoke is gone it is remembered no more." That last view of life is from an essay written by a camper in that first English Camp.

But English Camp is not a heavy experience...it is often the highlight week of a camper's year, and more than one camper wrote of this first camp that it was the best week of his or her life..."the best of times."

English Camp offers an opportunity to grow in English through three hours of morning lessons with a native English speaker. The English experience extends throughout the day as campers mingle and play with Americans, and if the campers are bold, they will attempt to converse with their American guests.

Afternoons are filled with a rich variety of activities that vary from camp to camp, but which typically include American sports, rope courses, nature hikes, and crafts and workshops. Evenings have programs with music and dance, ice-breaker games, hearing the life stories of American Team members, camper led skits and drama, and one or two Czech guest presenters. One special guest this week was Czech television musical host star, Aleš Juchelka.

Saturday morning, Nancy and I picked up Jane and Natasha to drive to Pec pod Sněžkou, a small town at the base of the highest Czech mountain Sněžka, in the Krkonoše Mountains National Park of the Czech Republic. This region is to Czech people what Yellowstone National Park is to Americans…it is the nation's most esteemed natural pride. Many of our campers had never visited this park, so coming to English Camp offered the double anticipation of meeting Americans and experiencing nature that is respected with worshipful awe.

For our one week camp, we rented the exclusive use of a ski resort pension inn. Ski resorts are busy in the winter but available at bargain prices during the summer. The pension capacity was fifty and we were pleased to have exactly fifty for our first camp. Upon arrival, there was first the busy exploration of every corner of the inn, a breath taking look at the natural beauty surrounding us, finding one's assigned room and meeting roommates…we were mostly strangers to each other.

Next came the English Camp examination. For most campers this is an hour of high tension… Czech students live by their life-determining school examinations. This camp exam, however, has no pass or fail grades; it is an analysis on each camper's level of English expertise. In less than sixty minutes we know who are the beginners, the intermediates, and the advanced students. Students are assigned accordingly to their morning English groups and teachers; with the beginners together with a teacher and the same up to the advanced…six groups in all. Jane and

Natasha both tested 'advanced' and were in a group taught by Dewey, an American from Michigan.

Because English Camp has both beginners and advanced campers, nearly all that we do and say is translated. All instructions for meals or afternoon sports are given bilingually. In the evening programs, songs are translated and then sung in English. When Americans tell their stories of life, marriage, education, faith, and home, it is all translated. Each class is assigned a translator to assist the teachers and campers. Some things take twice as long this way, but it is all part of the splendid camp adventure.

That first Saturday evening we met as a group of near strangers, but most campers came with a friend they had talked into registering for camp. The first night is the icebreaker night, with joyful games and clever ways of meeting the American Team. Six American teachers came from Carney, Michigan; all of them were from the Carney Evangelical Free Church. Only one was a schoolteacher, the others a postal employee, nurse, pastor, engineer, and a homemaker. One couple brought a high school son who made a natural bridge between the American adults and Czech students.

What made this USA team special was their kindness, enthusiasm, flexibility, eagerness to explore Czech culture and cuisine, and especially their warmth and love for the campers. Try to imagine the hilarity of Americans and Czechs together singing and dancing to the Chicken Dance song. When this first night was over we were no longer a group of fifty strangers...we were a bonded camp group who liked each other and expected a fantastic seven days to come. Soon we would climb the giant mountain, play softball and Frisbee football, sing, clap and dance to "I Am Somebody," and to Audio Adrenaline's "Big House," "Get Down," and "A Mighty Good Leader is on the Way."

To accelerate and simplify friendly communication, a new name was given to me. While Americans are known for friendliness and informality in conversation, the Czech culture has two forms of addressing people, formal and informal; with formal the normal rule, informal is reserved for family and close friends. Being called "Mr. Lupton" by those I wished to be friends with, including campers, seemed a barrier, but the culture would not permit students and many adults to call me Dan. Some Czech and American leaders came up with a compromise that could be the envy of international politics. From this summer forward, in camps and high schools, I would be "Mr. Dan."

Sunday morning began the classes…every camper wondered what these would be like, and teachers wondered the same. At breakfast the six class lists were posted with campers, teachers, and room assignments, with our first class session beginning at nine o'clock.

Each morning consisted of three, 50-minute lessons that included grammar, vocabulary words, idioms, pronunciation helps, discussion questions, and…one Bible story.

Czech atheists are less afraid of religion than American atheists, or at least they are less openly opposed and hostile toward Christians. But most campers had never read, seen or held a Bible…this most important book of the last two to four thousand years. We had chosen five Bible stories connected to the life of Jesus. These stories were read as stories; the teacher would then review the vocabulary in the story to see what words were new and needed an explanation. Most teachers would turn the story into a drama with assigned roles and reenact the story as a one-act play. It was all a fine, fun, and non-threatening learning experience.

Except for Jane Vlčková. . . .

The story for this day was of Jesus meeting and calling some to be his student followers. This seemed safely benign and even a little like the first 24 hours of English Camp, where we met each other, and campers were assigned to be under a particular teacher. As the American Camp Leader, I was not a teacher, so I walked quietly around to see if all was going well, or if classes needed additional writing supplies and assistance. All seemed fine until someone ran to me with news that something needed my urgent attention. In Jane's group, something had happened to cause her to run from the class, and lock herself in a restroom.

"It was the worst of times." My best student friend and camper was so emotionally upset at English Bible time that she ran and hid herself in a lavatory. I felt sorry for her pain and couldn't imagine what caused it. My mind raced to the natural outcome of this: I easily imagined she was on her cell phone calling her parents to come get her. Soon many would know of our terrible English Camp and my growing friendship with this family would be fractured. Thus, I summed up my fears and worst case, but logically anticipated, scenario.

I soon learned that in class, teacher Dewey had "off-the-cuff" adlibbed the remark that "God is so powerful." Other students scarcely heard or noticed the words...it made no unusual impression on them. But for Jane, it set off an emotional or spiritual explosion that jettisoned her from her seat and the room itself.

Jane, however, did not seek a way out...did not call for her parents to come take her from the camp. After a few minutes she emerged from the restroom, talked to Jana, our Czech team leader, and courageously stayed in the camp. Nancy and I gave her extra attention with unpressured friendship. Jane and Natasha ate most meals at a table with Nancy and me. The week became more relaxed and fun day by day, hour by hour. We never discussed the events of that morning until weeks later.

Early in the week, Natasha whispered that Jane's birthday was Thursday. Nancy, Natasha and I conspired to devise some way to celebrate her birthday with a surprise party, or at least a surprise ten minutes at the evening meal. During a free time we went to the village below the camp, bought a couple small memento gifts in a souvenir store and looked for a decorated cake. This was not the kind of town to have a bakery with birthday cakes, but we did find tiny candles. We improvised with a Czech pastry and inserted the candles. On her 17th birthday, the whole camp sang "Happy Birthday" to Jane and she blew out the candles. The week with such a tense beginning had turned out nearly perfect in every other moment for Jane. It had been a week of light and hope and going in a good direction. Jane didn't know it, but this would not be her only birthday this week.

*   *   *

This elementary sounding rap poem has served a fun overview of English Camp. I've used it in school classrooms and in the camp booklet each camper receives.

A Sneak Peak of English Camp Rap

Summer is here and it's time for camp;
Soon I'll be talking like an English champ.
Amazing Grace from American fame;
It's the camp song; you've heard its name.

The American team is from the land of bears;
Michigan nature can have a few scares.
Adults and teens, Yanks of every style,
Native English teachers make my time worthwhile.

Mornings will be filled with new English words;
Hope we escape being a bunch of nerds.
All will be translated so I can relax;
Don't need to worry about missing any facts.

Included will be a story from the grand old book;
Might do me some good to take a look.
Discussion will be part of the daily routine.
Should make a lively classroom scene.

Afternoons filled with a variety of fun;
American sports and hiking on the run;
Crafts and workshops, camera and stage,
Camp Olympics will be the Thursday rage.

Music and dance the evening fare,
If you dance near me let your feet beware.
Stories will be told by leaders plenty,
Should be worth a pretty penny.

Food is great, vegetarian or meat,
And there's plenty of it, no need to cheat.
Friends old and gained are treasures of the week;
Welcome and enjoy! concludes our sneak peak.

By Dan Lupton

IV
He is There

By Jane

While on Saturday afternoon I unpacked my camp backpack and watched TV, on Sunday there was a more special thing to do...maybe a little bit frightening, too. That morning I was going to church. What would it be like? What would the people there be like? Was it a good place to be? Finally, I will see the church that organized English Camp, I thought to myself. I was a little nervous, but definitely full of expectations of what we would do and see there, as Mr. Lupton came to pick up Natasha and me and we headed for Litomyšl.

I had been to some churches before. Once as a child I was even at part of a Catholic Mass with a dear friend of our family, but I only remember I was so young that I did not understand what it was about and just wanted to play or leave soon. Another time, I attended a funeral of my grandpa's relatives in an old Protestant church. Since that time I had not been in a church at all, except to attend a concert or guided tour.

When we came to the place where the church service was going to be - it was a hotel because the people from the church and the campers would not have fitted into the church building - my curiosity even increased. I was at church...the beautiful large hotel hall did not look like the Catholic churches I was used to, or sometimes fascinated by, or scared of, but I was still at church and I felt good there. I remember people's smiling faces, polite and friendly greetings, kind looks from the elderly, questions about our Camp experience, Mr. Lupton's message, talking to Irena, Natasha and Jakub, and also crying. I think I started crying at some point when I was talking to Irena. She had been explaining something about God to me.

That afternoon after church was very enjoyable - we had a lot of delicious food and again I was surprised at the people's kindness and friendliness. I felt very welcome and accepted, like at Camp. There was also Camp music and dancing. As I danced, I realized in surprise that it was a dance for God. I did not mind, but did not want to think too deeply about this very fact. I was still an unbeliever after all.

The whole afternoon was a great time and then we had to say goodbye to our hospitable hosts and some campers who were from far away and leaving. I had gotten used to being around people and could not imagine how I would return to my old life again. I actually could not believe Camp was over!

When I arrived back home from church that afternoon, there was hardly anything to do. I wandered about our house back and forth. I did not feel very much like talking to anyone. That night I was going bowling with the Americans who were staying with families around town. I tried reading a book and listening to music, but it soon stopped amusing me because I was so full of experiences from Camp and the camp-church event that I just had to think of it all the time. I thought of the people, the classes, the games and the songs I sang with such joy - even though I did not believe in God. However, now I knew he existed. During Camp, I could see him being there with us, which was also true about the church service I had just been at. I could not explain it to myself, but since I had run out of the classroom at Camp in tears, his existence had become more real to me. I sensed he was at Camp and church, watching over us. And I felt his presence even yet. This sense followed me wherever I went and it was becoming unbearable. Minutes became like hours. Hours like days. I could not find peace. I knew he saw me and what is more, he was waiting for something. Or for somebody?

It was Sunday afternoon and I sat down to eat. Our house was so quiet. Not even our neighbors were outside. Nothing was happening. The sun was shining, but there were long periods of shadows and a light breeze. I had some soup only to realize that I did not have much of an appetite. I felt again he was there and could no longer ignore him. I was weighed down by this strange situation and the fact he was there and felt so embarrassed for all the things I had done. I knew he could see me wholly; a girl weighed down by her guilt. I couldn't hide from him. I had to face him.

Maybe it will help if I talk to God, came to my mind, and I moved the plate aside. Suddenly it was as if I was standing on a crossroads with three paths leading from it. The left path meant my old life, the way I lived before Camp; the middle path was the way I was now - in between; and the right path...it brought something I did not know anything about. It was life with God. Life with God. Life with God? What does it mean? What is this about?

I knew I could not go back to the life I led before Camp, the life that was so hopeless. I could not even stay where I was because I just knew I could not bear to live this way either. I was standing before the path of life with God, and I remembered that people often said in their testimonies, that they were aware they knew nothing about it, but wanted to try it. From Camp, I knew God was good. I remembered that Jesus died for our sins on the cross and whoever comes to him receives Eternal Life. Whoever... that means anybody...even me. I had learned all these things, but I had to tell him and accept them personally, because you can know about many things but your heart can still be distant.

At that very moment, I decided to try it with God like in Psalm 34.8: *"Taste and see that the Lord is good."* I knew I should pray. It is not easy to come to God when you are so heavy loaded, though. I felt guilty and ashamed. I felt God was so holy that I could hardly stand before him. Would he forgive me even those sins that I found so big and so huge they were almost impossible to forgive?

Then I overcame my pride and started talking to God. I could not even speak for tears as I addressed him and told him about the things from my past which were like wounds all over my body, deep under the flesh and burning so much. I must have been sitting and praying there in tears for a long time. I saw that neither unhealthy relationships with boys, nor using tarot cards to know the future, or the decision to change oneself, or living according to oneself is right or fulfilling. As I confessed my guilt from the past, one by one, sins started falling off me, be it disobedience to my parents, bad thoughts, bad behavior, sins from my relationships, envy, pride and so many more things, which I could ever remember. As I prayed and told God about these things, I also asked him to forgive me. I told him I needed him and wanted to live for him. I also thanked him for his love; although I could not understand how it was possible he could love me. All this time through the prayer I could not stop crying. Some sins were also so hard to talk about and even naming them was not easy. I decided to rely on God's power forgiving me, even those sins I thought were so serious. When I finished my prayer I was feeling relieved. My wounds seemed to be healed. Still with closed eyes, I could see as if a baby was being born.

After this prayer, I looked up and felt very special. What just happened?

Wow! I really did it!

I looked around to find out if something had changed in the kitchen or outside. Still quiet. Nothing new. Just a little bit of sunshine came to the kitchen and tickled my nose. As time passed, I felt God's eye upon me and was very excited that he was now in my life. I still could not believe it had happened, but I was very grateful.

When I came to the bowling alley, there were some people from Camp and all the Americans from the team. I first kept all that had happened secret. I was going to tell individuals about it and I was waiting for the right opportunity. I wanted to tell Mr. Lupton first, because besides being my friend, he had invited me to Camp and had been helping me since he came to our school. Towards the end of the night, my friends told me Mr. Lupton was about to leave. I wished to tell him on this very day and was sorry he was already leaving for home. I caught up with him at the door. After I told him I was sorry he was leaving so soon I told him briefly: "Mr. Lupton, now you can consider me a Christian." At that moment I did not know what else to say, but Mr. Lupton understood. He hugged me, cried with joy, and told me that the whole Heaven was rejoicing, over me, a sinner repenting. They were having a party over me...a Heavenly Celebration!

After I told Mr. Lupton, the news spread quickly. People were so happy as I told them; some had tears of joy. Irena was there and she gave me a little book of the New Testament, which was my first Czech Bible. At Camp I had received an English Bible. When Mr. Lupton returned he brought me a little card, my "new birth certificate of a believer in Jesus" and I let him and Dewey sign it. Natasha was there too. She was happy too, but she did not believe yet.

On that day I was feeling the change in my life. I was happy that God loved me and I loved him too. There was just one thing I was unsure about. I was slowly becoming more nervous about telling my family...my grandparents, my parents, and my sister. I would see them soon. What should I say to them? How were they going to react? Would they accept it? My family was coming home from their holiday away. I was looking forward to them so much and praying God would give me words to explain to them I was now a Christian believer. I remember first visiting my grandparents on that day, to see them after Camp and tell them about this good news which I was so happy about.

I had always loved my grandparents. When my sister and I were little we spent a lot of time at their place. They lived only a few houses from us, in a tall apartment house like ours. How beautiful those days in our childhood were when we were walking on the sidewalk to our grandparents' with our mom watching over us from our window and granny expecting us in her window; both of them keeping an eye on us. We would play cards and other board games with our granny and have good talks with our grandpa, usually about history, literature and Czech. Whereas, granny would spend a lot of time in their wonderful smelling kitchen (she would always cook something delicious), grandpa could always be found typing something on his typing machine, and later on his computer, in his room full of books. That is where I found my liking for books.

I have only good memories of our time spent with them, time which belonged to our sunny childhood. When I was with our grandparents and our whole family, even as a little child, I realized how safe I felt, how happy. I thought it was a matter of course. Now when looking back, I am aware how blessed I was to have all of this.

Well, grandpa was the first I approached and told about my faith in Christ. He seemed to like it and was happy. I knew he used to be a believer himself when he was as young as me, or still was. He started talking about going to church when he was a teenager and about a choir he was part of. He was a member of a conservative Protestant church (Církev českobratrská). I hoped he was still a believer. I remembered grandpa saying something before he went to bed when I used to sleep in his room, when my sister and I were sleeping at our grandparents, which I thought was a silent prayer. Later grandpa even showed me his photo from his confirmation and his Bible.

I also told granny, whom I knew was Catholic and who was also happy to hear my story of faith. Granny said from that time on she was praying for our family. That was very encouraging to hear. My granny and grandpa were believers from two different denominations. Although they both believed, faith did not become a family thing. Instead, both of them kept their faith very personally.

Now with both of my dear grandparents knowing I was a Christian, I was facing the arrival of my parents and sister. They were supposed to come very soon. I had been praying that they would understand, and they would not object.

We had always had very nice relationships in our family. My parents were a great couple that matched each other in every possible way. We had experienced such wonderful moments together and we knew each other as well as nobody else. The last thing I wanted would be to put a strain on our relationship. How should I tell them? How should I approach it? Well…when I told my sister, she thought I was just making fun, maybe that it was just a joke. Maybe she thought I was foolish. It was too crazy to believe, too incredible. My mom thought I was part of a sect and in danger. She was afraid for me. All these reactions were understandable and I was never mean to them for thinking that. When I told my dad he took it open-mindedly and even started asking me questions about my faith and God. It was great that he was interested, and I often realized I needed to read the Bible more and look for answers to my own questions.

By Dan

In our blue Czech Skoda Fabia auto for the return to Svitavy, Jane and Natasha, Nancy and I laughed again over the Czech tradition skit night and other wonderful memories in our mental luggage of English Camp. We were friends still, and even more so. Surviving rough moments will bond friendships as much as enjoying the happier shared experiences, and this week provided both. We had survived Jane running out of the classroom in a panic at the beginning of camp, had sung, learned, played, danced and celebrated for seven days, and now we liked and trusted each other more than before.

Before leaving the majestic Pec pod Sněžkou, the campers were invited to a camp-focused church service the next morning in the church called in Czech, the Církev bratrská Litomyšl, which means the Brethren Church of Litomyšl. In the church service we sang and danced to several of our favorite camp songs. With most of the camp songs, we had developed a choreography that was fun to dance to and entertaining to watch. This would be a new experience for everyone, since no regular church member had ever before danced to music or witnessed such in a Sunday morning service; and since most of the campers had never been to a church service. Svitavy residents are accustomed to entering church buildings for community Christmas concerts and civic programs, but few have attended a Catholic Mass or a Protestant church service.

This would be a ground breaking, ice breaking, glass breaking, outside the box Sunday. All those idioms mean doing or attempting something new and different. To turn a typical church service on its head even more, we showed photos of the week's highlights, heard another life story or testimony from an American, and I brought the morning message or sermon as it is often called.

To the credit and bravery of the campers, most of them came and timidly entered a building like they were breaking some law and hoped to not be rebuked. To the credit of the members of the Církev bratrská Litomyšl, no one gasped or choked or fled when we sang and danced in the front of the church. My memory is that they applauded and the campers suddenly felt relaxed and welcome.

Soon it was time for me to bring a Bible oriented message, which is the custom in churches. I opened with these words...

"I wish to share with you what 90% of the Czech Bohemian and Moravian people once knew and believed. It was the center of their faith and they taught it to the world. America became a Christian nation because Moravian Brethren came to the American colonies and taught this message."

Today, we meet a man in spiritual confusion – there is a lot of that going on in the world still today. This man lacked the ability to understand God. His name was Nicodemus. Nicodemus was a religious man, but being religious is not the same as being spiritually alive and knowing God. Let's listen to this conversation in the New Testament, the Gospel [Good News] written by John.

[John 3.1-4, NLT] *"There was a man named Nicodemus, a Jewish religious leader who was a Pharisee. ² After dark one evening, he came to speak with Jesus. "Rabbi," he said, "we all know that God has sent you to teach us. Your miraculous signs are evidence that God is with you." ³ Jesus replied, "I tell you the truth, unless you are born again, you cannot see the Kingdom of God." ⁴ "What do you mean?" exclaimed Nicodemus. "How can an old man go back into his mother's womb and be born again?"*

You need to remember that I have only half the time I'd normally use since all must be said twice, first by me in English and a second time translated into Czech. I rather like the freedom to say a phrase and then prepare for the next sentence while the translation is happening. But paring a 30-minute talk to 15 minutes can be a challenge.

So I explained the conversation between Jesus and Nicodemus with this story.

Recently I stood by a Czech cottage well – an old fashioned pump well. I asked if the pump worked and no one knew. From inside the cottage we got a bucket of water and I poured some into the well to prime it, and I began to pump. Soon out came a dark, reddish, rusty, dirty water. I pumped and pumped and all that ever came was disgusting water we didn't dare to drink.

What if I'd said, "I know how to fix this bad water? I need a liter of paint." And what if I'd painted that pump? Would I now get clean water?

You would say, "Only a fool would paint a pump to cure bad water." It isn't new paint but a new water source that is needed. Man's dirty well is described in the Bible: [Mark's Gospel, 7.21, NLT] *"Out of a person's heart come evil thoughts, sexual immorality, theft, murder, adultery, greed, wickedness, deceit, lustful desires, envy, slander, pride, and foolishness. All these come from within; they are what defile you."*

What we need is not an external change – a coat of paint. We need a change at the very source of life. We need a new spiritual birth that gives a new heart.

The new birth is God's Holy Spirit creating in us God's nature. John's friend the Apostle Peter explained it this way: *"you may become partakers of the divine nature"* [2 Peter 1.4, NKJV].

Every person shares through DNA the nature of his or her parents. I look in the mirror and say, "Hi dad." I look like my earthly father, and I often think and feel like him. His nature is in me. But more often I look up and say, "Hi my God & Father." Because I've been born again, I have his nature and know in my heart what he loves and feels."

Soon the meeting time was finished and we went outside to eat. For the hour immediately after church, we had advertised a "Potluck" Lunch. A "Potluck" is when all the people bring something to the table. In Medieval times, there would have been a great Pot hanging over a fire and guests would have added their meat or potatoes or vegetables... whatever they had to throw in. Lacking such a pot, we set up tables to receive our contributions of plates and bowls of home cuisine. Since the meal is unplanned, what happens is "luck." In my life memories of such meals, these have always been good luck and great experiences... I always left a potluck smiling and satisfied.

It was late July and the weather was as perfect at it gets in the Czech Republic...the low 20s, or the mid-70s for Americans. What a meal! The potluck was a feast. Many in the church had brought grills and charcoal with meat to cook and share with others. There was a variety of salads and vegetables...even Czech men and boys are learning to tolerate these. But the church ladies especially shine with their desserts, all looking picture perfect. Someone had made two cakes and decorated the tops with white frosting and red currents and blueberries. One cake was the visual image of the Czech Flag and the other was the American Flag. Side by side, these reminded us of the friendship between the American church volunteers and the Czech camp team and church.

As lunch was ending the music was cranking up. In the garden by the church building, we sang and danced to our favorite songs one more time. When we were done with this it was time to go home, but this group of campers, atheists and followers of Christ, were bonded as one and didn't want the camp experience to end. Someone had the bright idea of going bowling in the evening...extending the fun of English Camp... not letting it end.

At 6:00pm, we met at the AMD Moto bowling alley... not all the campers, but 20 or 25 of the original group. I have my good nights and not so good nights with a bowling ball in my hand. This was not one of my better bowling experiences...I've forgotten my scores, probably intentionally. But the night would end perfectly. All were having fun bowling, cheering every pin knocked down by anyone. Some campers were bowling for the first time. What a week of firsts...first English Camp, first church service, first time bowling.

Saturday through Saturday, plus Sunday made nine days of English Camp. I needed to take the American team back to Prague the next morning, so I was one of the first to put my bowling ball away and my street shoes back on. I greeted everyone again, waved my goodbyes and headed to the door.

With my hand on the exit door, Jane hurried up to me. "Mr. Dan, I have one more thing to tell you before you leave. You may now consider me a Christian believer." Even as I write this, I choke up with the emotions I felt at that moment. But instead of saying something sensible, I answered, "That is wonderful! Have you told God yet?"

Jane knew what I meant and told me, "Oh yes, I prayed for the first time this afternoon. I told God all my sins and invited and welcomed Jesus to my life as Savior and Leader."

I hugged her and asked, "May we tell the others? The Americans will leave in the morning and they will want to rejoice with you." I reminded her that even the angels of Heaven were rejoicing in a party celebrating her new life of faith. So we told all the Americans and not a few of our Czech friends. The unbelievers were a bit confused but continued bowling and didn't mind as they observed the hugs and tears of joy.

For the morning church service, I had prepared 'Birth Certificates.' When one is born physically, the delivering doctor will prepare a birth certificate for the state. I knew that when one trusts and welcomes God and Jesus, this person has another kind of birth…a spiritual birth. The thought came that such a person should have a Spiritual Birth Certificate. The one I prepared included the words Jesus spoke from John 3, a place for the new believer's name and signature, and a line for a witness to sign and date. Why I had this certificate at a bowling party I don't know, but I did, and I suddenly remembered it. We completed this certificate for Jane as a souvenir memory of this day.

In the week that Jane's 17th birthday was almost forgotten, she now had two birthdays and two birthday celebrations.

The wall that hindered our friendship did have a way through. The wall that separated Jane from God had crumbled, been swept away and was forever gone.

V

Russian Nesting Dolls

By Jane

Many Christians say that when they started believing in God, they were so happy all the time... they always felt like smiling, almost jumping with joy... Something like that actually happened to me too! I suddenly had hope in my life and this hope was something I did not know before. I was filled with expectations of my newfound life and deeply at peace with God. Often I sought opportunities to read my New Testament.

I started reading Matthew because it seemed logical to me to start with the first book of the four Gospels. I remembered Mr. Dan saying the four Gospels were like four stories about the events of the life of Jesus, and though different in style, they were all about him. Sometimes when I was reading though, I did not fully understand all that I found there.

I had responded to God's calling at Camp and after Camp without actually knowing much about him. Now I wanted to get to know him better and learn more about his character.

A few days later, Natasha told me that she had believed in God, too. I was even happier now that there were the two of us together again. We both liked to meet with Mr. Dan and talk to him about various things and faith.

I remember that Natasha and I came to Mr. Dan's one afternoon and he gave us a brochure about certain facts that happen at the moment of salvation. Some of them are being forgiven, accepted as children of God and heavenly citizens, and justified in God's eyes, which we did not understand even after Mr. Dan's explanation. He said we would see what it meant later and he was right because the time came when I realized that God looks at us as if we had not committed any sin, because we have believed that Jesus paid for our faults. Talks with Mr. Dan were always very encouraging to me. After my conversion, we continued to communicate together per email and got to see each other at school, and also in another place where I had started going...it was church.

I knew there was some tension in my family caused by the fact I was now a believer. And when I asked my parents to allow me to go to church the next Sunday following English Camp church service, they agreed, but they did not wish I would go there the next time. But what happened was that the next Sunday, I very much wanted to go to church again and the Sunday after next again. The messages from the pastor interested me and helped me learn more about God. It was by God's grace that my parents mostly agreed. I appreciated their approval all the more because I knew several young people whose parents did not allow that.

The people in the church were also very friendly and I soon became friends with many. I was encouraged by people coming to me and asking me how I was doing. I felt I was part of them, God's family. I felt like I did at English Camp, since there were many Christians who were so welcoming, and who showed me their kindness.

When I asked my parents the next time if I could go to church, they seemed to be worried and said I should not go there. I think they were still afraid that I was part of a strange community and they did not want much of the people's influence on me. I tried to explain to my parents that it was no sect, that although it may sound crazy to somebody, it was a Christian church where we sang, prayed, and listened to the pastor's sermon and it was okay. But I also did not want to disobey. I was thankful that many times they finally approved, but I know they did not like it very much.

I found myself praying for my family a lot and asking God to let them believe in him too. I also tried to be my best, and I wished for him to change me and make me the person he wanted me to be. I was aware that especially cleaning my room sometimes got out of my control. Years later, though, my sister testified that she could not believe how much different I was compared to before, and started wondering why that was.

I really wanted to do good things for people around me. I was a spiritual baby, trying to walk with the Lord and getting to know him. I was stumbling at times and realized very often that in many situations I needed to think first and then speak, not to hurt anyone with what I said. I would read the Bible, but sometimes I had days without reading it and just living on what I read the previous day and still musing about it.

I do not remember anymore how it happened but Mr. Dan, Natasha, and I started talking about baptism. Mr. Dan suggested we could do Bible classes with Irena and Jakub, because it was easier for us to do it in Czech. I still did not feel I could understand it in English and appreciated that idea. We went there several times; we talked about how God had been working in our lives and we also asked him to lead us and let us be a light to our relatives. We also talked about magic and witchcraft. It was then that I learnt those were evil. We then prayed for one of our friends engaging in it to see that future-telling is not good and will not help anyone. I also confided in Irena that I had engaged in witchcraft myself by listening to tarot cards and the healer whose medicine I was still taking... She told me I should talk to God about this particular thing again if I had not confessed it yet, and make a decision that I would never return to it. So that night I told God again, and rejected any activities like that.

That night, however, it got really complicated. I started feeling really scared and was not sure if God had forgiven me everything. Doubts were coming to mind – not about his existence, but whether he had really forgiven me all my sins. I talked about some of these doubts with Mr. Dan, Irena, and Jakub, and received messages assuring me God was faithful in keeping his promises – and as it is written "Who has the Son has life, who does not have the Son of God does not have life," from 1 John 5.12, it is so, even though our feelings tell us something else.

School started again in September and Natasha and I still attended the Bible classes. Soon after the beginning of school, we realized we had so much to do for school that we sometimes did not even read the Bible or do the homework from our Bible study. It was in those days that Natasha told me she had realized she actually did not believe. She said she was excited about Camp, all our American friends, even me believing, and she thought she believed too. But time showed it was just a temporary feeling. Her family might not have approved either, so that was another reason why she had decided to quit. This was happening and I was unable to do anything about it. I was disappointed, mainly for her and hoped she would come back again. I remember telling Mr. Dan who knew that Natasha did not have it very easy in her family, and he said God would never quit on her. I miss her.

At school things were becoming more serious for us because we were supposed to elect subjects that would help us prepare for our final examinations and university entrance exams. We were in school almost all day long, spending a lot of time together. My intention was now to behave well to others. I hoped that by doing good, even to people who I knew would only misuse others and did things which were not right, I could improve my relationship with them, so they could see I did not want to be against them.

There were some people around me with whom it was challenging for me to get along with – but I saw God giving me enough patience with them, and even seeing that there was also something good about them, even though I was first quite unwilling to see that. I tried to overcome the difficulties of our relationship, trying to guard my tongue and not say anything negative about them. But several times I failed. I think that sometimes I must have sounded like a hypocrite to them when saying the opposite of what I would have said or thought in the previous years. Using cheat sheets also did not seem honest to me, as before.

That school year was quite difficult, but I could see Jesus helping me through my days and I appreciated it so much. Although my family might have thought at first that becoming a believer would distract me from my studies, I knew I had his help even in studying and I did very well at school. There were days when his help became so visible to me it was impossible to overlook. And there were so many demonstrations of his taking my side and strengthening me.

I did not manage to read the Scriptures every day... but had more and more questions, though. One of those that troubled me a lot was: How could God allow evil things to happen? God is good, so why does he let bad things happen to people? I was thinking a lot about people in concentration camps or people dying in wars. I learned from Mr. Dan that if God stops one powerful leader from doing evil, he also has to stop every other person from doing bad things, including you and me...

Another question I thought about: What is the sin against the Holy Spirit? It might have worried me even more than the first question because it says all can be forgiven, except for this one sin. If I'd committed it, then I was where I had been before I believed.

I found the verse about this sin when I was reading Matthew. Bad thoughts filled my mind – thoughts about God, that he was bad, which I absolutely disagreed with and all this bothered me. The thoughts got so aggressive at times, that I found myself calling on the Lord in despair to help me out of that. I could not believe I was actually thinking these thoughts. At one point I was even asking myself: Can God forgive me all of these thoughts? Does he still love me even after this? I was depressed and confused. I was struggling with thoughts that were saying the real opposite of what I was thinking of him. I experienced what is written in 1 Peter 5.8, that ... Satan is walking around as a roaring lion ready to devour us. My thinking about this sin threw me off so much that I could not read the Bible anymore and just had to think about that all the time. Was I completely lost? I decided to share this with Mr. Dan in an email and ask him for help and explanation.

Dear Mr. Dan,

I have a spiritual problem. I am very sorry to bother you with this. But you were one of the first ones who I thought of when I was wondering who to ask. I know that I have talked to my friends about the thing I want to ask you about but I have forgotten the answer. What is sin against the Holy Spirit? When I was falling asleep this afternoon suddenly I thought of this and I do not know how it was possible but I said to myself - if I were to sin against him I would have to say something like the Holy Spirit is silly. I know I should not have thought about it but the thought came and I said this sentence without profoundly thinking about its meaning. I did not want to hurt him and as soon as I said this sentence I was sorry about this. Immediately I remembered that a year ago Jakub told me, that nobody can be forgiven such a sin. Does it mean that if somebody sins this way they cannot be in the family of God? I am sorry for these questions. I tried to apologize to God but what if he cannot forgive me?

Hi Jane,

Let me quickly assure you that you did not commit an unpardon-able sin against the Holy Spirit. If your father heard you say you thought he was silly, would he disown you? My children have said worse about me. But I still loved them and knew they loved me, even if in the heat of emotion they said something hurtful.

What you did is called grieving the Holy Spirit.

Ephesians 4.29: "Do not let any unwholesome talk come out of your mouths, but only what is helpful for building others up according to their needs, that it may benefit those who listen. 30 And do not grieve the Holy Spirit of God, with whom you were sealed for the day of redemption. 31 Get rid of all bitterness, rage and anger, brawling and slander, along with every form of malice. 32 Be kind and compassionate to one another, forgiving each other, just as in Christ God forgave you."

Please notice the great security and love which God gives you even as you grieved God's Spirit. You are still sealed to him, even as you grieve him. I think we most often grieve those who love us the most.

Here is a quote from an Internet source[1]:

> *"To understand what it means to 'grieve' the Spirit, we must first understand that this is a personality trait. Only a person can be grieved, therefore, the Spirit must be a person in order to have this emotion. Once we understand this aspect, we can better understand how he is grieved, mainly because we, too, are grieved. Ephesians 4.30 tells us that we should not grieve the Spirit. Let's stay in the passage to understand what Paul wants to tell us. We can grieve the Spirit by living like the pagans [4.17-19], by yielding to our sin nature [4.22-24], by lying [4.25], by anger [4.26-27], by stealing [4.28], by cursing [4.29], by bitterness [4.31], by being unforgiving [4.32], by sexual immorality [5.3-5]. To grieve the Spirit is to act out in a sinful manner, whether it is in thought and deed, or in thought only."*

So here is what you do about this. First you read 1 John 1.9: "If we confess our sins, he is faithful and just and will forgive us our sins and purify us from all unrighteousness." Then you tell the Father, the Son and the Holy Spirit you really trust and

---

1 Found at http://www.gotquestions.org/grieve-quench-Holy-Spirit.html.

love them [3 in one] and that you feel greatly sorry for what you said. "Dear Father, and also Son and Holy Spirit, I thought and said some things that brought grief to your heart. I long to be the one you look at and rejoice over. I thank you that one year ago today you celebrated my coming into your family. Please forgive what I said and celebrate me again as your child. I wish to bring glory and joy to you, even as you love and care for me every day. Thank you for this one great year and I pray that you will lead me everyday. Amen."

The very serious sin against the Holy Spirit, the one you mentioned, is when an unbeliever says that the things God does is the work of the devil. It is to so reject God and his works that it turns everything 180. The sum is that the most serious sin is such unbelief that it rejects God and ascribes evil to him. It is a heart that is hardened in unbelief and hatred toward God. We can look at that more if you wish, but mainly I wanted to quickly deal with your grief and fear.

Who loves you with everlasting love? God, including the Holy Spirit. Even now. He knows how weak we are and how much the enemy wants to reclaim us. You are sealed to him. You are born again. That what you said grieves you, also is additional proof of your new birth and relationship to God, as his daughter.

Yours,

Mr. Dan,

When struggling with these bad thoughts I wondered at one point whether I was not also struggling with my pride. I tried to throw it away and humble myself before God, calling for help.

Hi, Mr. Dan,

I think I may have one more problem. Sometimes I find myself thinking about something I do not want to think about at all. But how do you think I should get rid of such questions and thoughts? I have asked God to help me with this and He did for some time but then the thoughts returned. I am sorry again that I bother you. Jane

Hi, Jane,

Please know that you have a Father who loves you. Also, you have an enemy who remembers the day he lost you from his slave kingdom. Slave owners in America and Europe sent out evil people who tracked runaway slaves to catch them and bring them back to the plantation. This can't happen to you, but the enemy who lost for sure on the day Jesus rose from the grave, still tries. Read the last half of Ephesians 6. Also, Ephesians 4 gives help with your questions. It talks about putting off the old and putting on the new.

To better answer your question I need to know, not the details, but the nature of your thought problems.

Are these thoughts that trouble you...

1. *History...memories of things you've done in the past?*
2. *History...memories of hurtful destructive things others have done or said to you?*
3. *Relational thoughts of anger, resentment, hatred toward others?*
4. *Temptations toward greed or lust?*
5. *Jealousy?*
6. *Thoughts toward God of why he allowed something?*

Please help me to know the kind of issue you are dealing with.

In the meantime, read Ephesians 4 and 6. And maybe Psalm 51.

Love and prayers,

Mr. Dan

I thought about the origin of these bad thoughts. Is it possible that they were from evil? I found out that some of the people I knew were sending me energy, so I asked them not to do it anymore. Who knows if that had something to do with it? I also gradually stopped taking the medicine I had received from the healer about whose origin I actually did not know much. After doing so, I felt weaker at some point, but I tried to persevere.

I was suffering from the illness anyway – as time showed the energy or the medicine did not make my tonsil problem any better, and after the experience with bad thoughts, I made a strong decision that I never wanted to receive energy from anyone else, only from him.

By Dan

Jane was no longer an atheist. She had met and experienced God who had accomplished something mysteriously marvelous in her soul. But what happened and what is she now to do? How will friends and family treat her when she tells them of the new things in her life? As for me, how am I to be involved and how do I feel?

I felt elated, like a mom who has just given birth to a healthy child. Well, I'm a guy, but I imagine a new mother, while feeling exhausted, would also be entirely exhilarated at the miracle wonder of birth. Nancy and I celebrated Jane's spiritual birth with euphoric tears; we rejoiced with the angels of heaven. Maybe you've held a newborn child, or visited a couple holding a baby. Is there a happier place on this globe than with a family and their newly born child?

To a materialist atheist, the concept of a spiritual birth is foreign beyond comprehension. But atheism isn't always materialistic. A brand of Czech atheism is known as "Somethingism." Somethingism avers, "I don't believe in God, but I believe there is something more, something spiritual around us." A Somethingist might mention feeling extra energy in a forest, or might dabble with astrology and tarot cards. A Somethingist atheist could be interested in a spiritual birth.

Deep inside it is normal to believe there is something more...God or something godlike. It is both intuitive and reasonable. A 2000-year old famous letter summed it up well: *"The basic reality of God is plain enough. Open your eyes and there it is! By taking a long and thoughtful look at what God has created, people have always been able to see what their eyes as such can't see: eternal power, for instance, and the mystery of his divine being"* [Romans 1.18-20, ML].

I wondered if Jane's friends and relatives were materialist atheists or something-thingist atheists. I think she was never a Somethingist. A Somethingist thinks about spiritual things and Jane told me that in her first 17 years she couldn't recall one conversation in her home about God and whether he is, or not, and that prayer had never been mentioned.

Jane's experience in atheism was a twin to that of the Pardubice political leader who represented the regional government at the cornerstone dedication of a Litomyšl church building. After kind words of congratulations and wishing the church well, this elected leader bared his heart in a moment of transparent clarity with the unscripted words, "I have no faith and I don't know how to live without faith."

That was the conflict you read in Jane's description of her early teen years. She had no faith and didn't know how to build her life since it lacked any purposeful or rational foundation. She cast about in a variety of activities and relationships; she listened to the voices calling her to live one haphazardly risky way or another; she sampled the worldly teen culture in its attempts at pleasure and in the pursuit of happiness; and all of these left her with a bitter aftertaste of disappointment, disgust, and a vague inexplicable sense of guilt.

Deciding she would not follow the teen culture down the dead-end road of sensuality and popularity, she turned her life energies to the more respectable and practical pursuit of a quality education that would gain her a university acceptance letter and lead to a fifty-year career. If she must learn German and English, she would be the best student. When assigned to a research project, she learned all she could and wrote a one hundred four page paper, single-spaced. I doubted that her teacher did more than a brief scan of this extensive project. When the city of Svitavy was planning its 750th anniversary celebration and needed an art logo for this historic event. A contest was promoted to see which citizen could design the best logo; Jane's entry was the winner and she gained her "fifteen minutes of fame" through this.

She won the respect of students and her school for her achievements, won the acclaim of the community for her art, and after the applause ended, even this appeared as vanity, something mist-like to appear and vanish and be of no lasting worth. Jane thought, "Fifty years after I die no one will remember that I ever lived; why am I working so hard to get good grades in school?" Or to quote another, *"Everything is meaningless—like chasing the wind"* [Ecclesiastes 2.17, NLT].

At English Camp, Jane met people who had chosen a different and new path, a life direction foreign to Czech teen culture. It was a life full of purpose because it was planned and led by the Father above who designed Jane for all he had in mind for her. Jane went straight from materialist atheist to a relationship with Jesus as her Shepard Savior and with God as her Father. She no longer would grasp for the wind... she would live every day with purpose, the purpose for which she was created and born. All she needed was a spiritual awakening and God would provide even this for her.

Jane's spiritual birth was the product of God's Holy Spirit. *"That which is born of the [human] flesh is flesh; and that which is born of the Spirit is spirit"* [John 3.6, KJV]. Just consider how much a child contributes in being conceived, nurtured in the womb for nine months, and then born? A child is 100% the product of two parents. A baby's part is only to feel squeezed and to put the head in the right direction [hopefully]. Jane's only part in her spiritual birth was to recognize her need and express it in repentance and faith. Jesus explained the new birth to a teacher named Nicodemus and then summed it up for all of us this way: *"For God so loved the world that he gave his one and only Son, that whoever believes in him shall not perish but have eternal life"* [John 3.16, NIV].

The new birth can only be experienced this way: one trusts the Lord Jesus Christ to do what one cannot do for him/herself. God loves us; Jesus has already died and risen for us, and the Holy Spirit will work the change in our hearts. You and I become a child of God the moment we accept Christ and believe in him to forgive past crimes and lead us in a healthier path.

One of the first things I desired Jane to understand was her new position and all the riches that accompanied her new birth. When you and I were born physically we were placed in a family, given a name, clothed and fed, cleaned and bathed, protected from danger, made to feel secure and loved, photographed and bragged about, and became legal heirs. We weren't on probation…these were ours by birthright. That is the general plan, except that some parents break the model…no human dad or mom is perfect.

The question was, "Now that Jane has been spiritually born, what has she received of value with that?"

I gave Jane a small booklet titled "33 Things That Happen at the Moment of Salvation."

- Forgiven
- Child of God
- Having access to God
- A part in the Eternal Plan of God
- Reconciled
- Justified
- Placed "in Christ"
- Heavenly citizenship
- Within the "much more" care of God
- Redeemed

- A living relationship with God
- Adoption
- Delivered from the power of darkness
- God's inheritance
- Complete in him
- Possessing every spiritual blessing

The full list is doubly amazing. It's like opening a traditional Russian nesting doll. One holds the doll and thinks, "This is beautiful and I'll enjoy this doll all my life." I've been forgiven and I'll be forever grateful for this. Then the holder discovers that the doll opens up and nesting inside is a second doll as beautiful as the first. Jane discovered she was also now a child of God. This is just as beautiful as being forgiven. And then a third doll and a fourth, and it seems each doll increases in splendor. Jane had access to God at any time and she was in God's Eternal Plan. Her birthright grows in splendor with each discovery.

The largest set of Russian nesting dolls is a 51-piece set, hand painted by Youlia Bereznitskaia in 2003. Here's the updated news on the booklet "33 Things That Happen at the Moment of Salvation." It is incomplete. I've read this list as containing more than 51 benefits that accompany a Spiritual rebirth. It won't surprise you that the list of 33 [or 51+] comes from the Bible, the most important book of Czech and American history. I encouraged Jane to read the Bible.

Jane had been spiritually born and like any baby she was hungry and sought to be fed. *"As newborn babes, desire the pure milk of the Word that you may grow thereby"* [1 Peter 2.2, NKJV]. When we were born from our mom's womb, the first food that we were fed was milk. The reason is that milk, especially mother's milk, contains essential nutrients for the body's health and growth. God has milk...spiritual milk...that he wants his children to drink. It is the milk of the Word, the basics of the Bible.

After English Camp and before the next school term Jane sent me this note. *"You asked me what in the Bible I was reading - it is the second time I have read John. First I read it in Czech, then I watched the Gospel of John film and now I am reading it in English in the English Bible which I received at the camp. Then I am going to read Luke."* Jane was already no longer spoon-fed...she was feeding herself in a most satisfying way.

She read the New Testament bilingually, which would confirm the dynamic stories from two sources with each language adding its linguistic nuances. Jane also had a third source in the Gospel of John movie, which added the visual impact while using the biblical script. Reading the Bible gives answers to questions one hadn't previously thought of, but it may also raise questions one doesn't know how to find the answers to. One of Jane's early questions was: *"Mr. Dan, I have just one "heavy" question which is lying on my back and troubling me very much. The question is: How could God allow Nazi Germans to kill people in concentration camps? As far as I know most of the victims were Jews who believed in God, so how is it possible? Thank you for thinking about it, Jane."*

Jane's question, I explained to her, was about where God should draw the line on human evil. We are outraged over such huge international evil as she asked about, angry at our own corrupt government leaders, upset with dishonest local business and social issues, annoyed with relatives who lie and slander, but are typically content with our own faults. I explained to Jane that if God stops Hitler, he must stop other government leaders around the world from destroying people, must stop local government leaders from corruption, must stop business leaders from cheating people, must stop abusive parents from harming children, and must stop you and me from doing inappropriate and destruction behavior. That would end human freedom and accountability. I also said the day will come when Jesus will indeed return and end all of this evil, including our own.

The way Jane asked her Hitler question is universal, but also especially Czech in nature. Czechoslovakia suffered under the murderous Nazi regime and nearly all its Jewish population were exterminated. It also suffered through hundreds of years of Hapsburg oppression and more recently under communism. More than a few would say they currently suffer under capitalism. Bohemians and Moravians understandably learned to view evil as something from the outside that is imposed on them.

That remains the current view. Evil is a corrupt politician and all politicians are corrupt. Evil is an unjust employer who uses, underpays, and fires people. Evil is a mean and unfair teacher. Evil is a child abuser. Evil is found everyplace one looks...except within one's self. One should never look into a mirror that would reveal that, *"The heart is deceitful above all things, and it is exceedingly corrupt: who can know it"* [Jeremiah 17.9, ASV]?

Days after Jane asked the global evil question, she asked the personal evil question. She was alarmed over what she saw when she looked inside herself. For a while she was blinded to see herself as God's forgiven child and treasure. I encouraged her with promises such as: *"He has removed our sins as far from us as the east is from the west. The LORD is like a father to his children, tender and compassionate to those who fear him"* and *"If we confess our sins to him, he is faithful and just to forgive us our sins and to cleanse us from all wickedness"*, [Psalm 103.12 and 1John 1.9NLT]. Jane was soon free again; free from the pain of looking at her own life through a rear view mirror, and her face was radiantly beautiful again. Eyes tell the truth like a window on the soul.

Jane really enjoyed church, this young lady who had previously described churches as cold and unwelcoming. But maybe she meant the buildings...the word "church" in the Czech lands refers to the structure, and when people are intended, instead of the building, they are referred to as "brethren." Since our building was nothing to boast of in beauty, I'll restart with "Jane really enjoyed the brethren."

Her parents granted her wish to be free Sunday mornings to attend a meeting of singing and prayers and learning. Not all atheist parents are so generous. The kindness and liberality on their part would eventually turn to their own benefit and I've always been grateful that Jane was not confined and denied the freedoms they granted her.

Nancy and I arrived at Jane's home each Sunday morning, 30 minutes before church. Sunday was filled with brightness each time the door of her home opened and she came to the car beaming and eager for whatever our Father had planned for this morning. Music was usually a mixture of ancient hymns played on an organ and modern worship choruses played with guitars and sometimes drums. In the USA, few churches know the benefit of bringing something old and something new for people to sing. It works in the Czech churches because it also works in the wider culture, where students may enjoy an a Capella choral concert Friday night and a metal concert Saturday night.

Jane became my Sunday morning sermon translator whispering the message to me in English. It amazed me that a high school junior could hear the message in one language and simultaneously translate it to another. Jane was serving the Lord and us in this way, and from those days to now she has always found her greatest joy in serving others with love. Her life became the living reality of this, *"The only thing that counts is faith expressing itself through love"* [Galatians 5.6, NIV].

We taught Jane to pray, but she didn't need much guidance with this. Jane knew she had access to God and we taught her that God was never annoyed with her coming to him, that God smiled with pleasure whenever she wished to converse with him. God was her Father above…it was that simple. Jesus on the cross, opened the door for her to come freely and often to the Father.

Jane and I have prayed together… and individually… for so many things. It is amazing to see God at work in prayer. Prayer is far more than asking for things. Maybe you know someone who, when he calls or knocks, you wonder, "what does he need and what will he ask for this time?" So I encourage new believers to talk to the Lord about the beauties they see in nature, to expect God to rejoice and laugh with us in the upbeat and funny moments, to tell Father thank you for his goodness often.

I believe that God made you and this world because he is love. He created the planets, stars, and angels and found pleasure in these. But he still had more love to give. He created us to know him and have a Father-child relationship with him. He didn't create Adam and Eve and walk away from them. He made a daily date to visit them in the cool of the day [Genesis 2&3]. God made Adam and Eve, and you and me, to be much like him so we could relate to him and enjoy his love. Prayer can be much more than begging… it can be family time with Father above.

But we do ask for things, and God answers the prayers of newer believer quickly. Later, Father may ask them to be patient, to trust him and wait. But early in their Christian walk, he understands that former atheists need speedy confirmation of their new faith, especially in their prayers.

One of the things that the Czech believers easily learn is to arrange and tell their stories to others. Those who have been to an English Camp have heard both Czech and American Christians tell their stories of life and faith integration, including how they came to faith in Christ and how he has strengthened their lives. The memory of these stories becomes a model for the newer believers.

Jane has many opportunities to explain her journey from atheism to child of God. She has told her story to groups, relatives, campers, and schoolmates. On "Planes, Trains and Automobiles," [old movie title] Jane is asked about her faith...by strangers. Asked in stores and concerts, on sidewalks, at work and recreation...by those who know and appreciate her. Such opportunities are God arranged moments.

Christians have many such God moments and they come in many forms. I learned from my mentor friend, David Mains, to always be on the watch for God sightings, and I passed this wisdom on to Jane.

King David spoke and wrote of God's wonderful miracles and awe-inspiring deeds. *"Your faithful followers will praise you. They will speak of the glory of your kingdom; they will give examples of your power. They will tell about your mighty deeds"* [Psalm 145.10-12, NLT].

In lines that followed, the people who knew God praised him for his:

- Faithfulness in times of need;
- Graciousness in how he treated them;
- Helpfulness when they fell;
- Aid in lifting those with heavy burdens in life;
- Provision of food and the essentials of life;
- Satisfying the needs of the heart;
- Closeness to them so they felt his presence;
- Listening ears when they call to him, and his protection.

James teaches, *"Don't be deceived, my dear brothers and sisters. Every good and perfect gift is from above, coming down from the Father of the heavenly lights..."* [James 1.16, NIV]. What does he mean, *"don't be deceived?"* He means don't fool yourself into thinking, "what an amazing coincidence," or "I sure was lucky there."

I've provided instruction like this for many, including Jane: "I want you to look for evidence of God in your life. It could be that he guides you, provides for you, protects you, encourages you, enables you to serve others, and certainly answers your prayers. I hope you will soon tell me things like, "Oh, God is so good to me. Today he taught me this, and helped me in school, and guided my words in a great conversation with someone."

For seven years, most emails from Jane have contained God sightings. The exceptions were the brief business notes such as, "train arrives at six...will come immediately to club." But emails with paragraphs of thoughts, typically include Jane's notices and praise for what God is doing in her life. I doubt she consciously writes this way; it has become part of who she is and how she responds to God and life.

Instead of reaching back seven or eight years, here is a fresh note that came in as I write. "I am so happy that more and more people have been registering for Camp. I pray for Camp every day and believe God will use it for his glory. I also had to cry when I read that most of the people-campers are from Svitavy because Svitavy is also one of the things I have been lately praying for."

With that brief note, Jane is living her birthright place in God's family, is having prayer experiences with God, is telling her continuing story and is giving praise for a God sighting in an answer to prayer. I agree with a man named John who wrote, *"I have no greater joy than to hear that my children are walking in the truth"* [3 John 4, NIV].

VI
Courage Provided

By Jane

It was in these days that my grandpa started having problems with his eyesight and health. My family and I were very concerned about him. We hoped his state of health would improve, that his eyes would be better and so would his sore knees, but the opposite was true. It was going to get even worse.

In the fall of the same year, he suffered from pain only to be diagnosed with cancer months later. When I learned about that, I was devastated. I thought of him and was sorry for him. I could not believe that was happening. My grandpa was so seriously ill... My grandpa....

He then underwent surgery in the local hospital and we had to wait for the results. I decided to visit him one afternoon after school when he was still at the hospital. It was cold and it was getting dark.

When I entered the room grandpa was sitting on his bed. Only a warm yellow light from the washbasin area lighted the room. Grandpa seemed to be in a good mood, talking to an old patient across the room. They had done surgery on grandpa a day before. I felt like crying when I saw the infusion in his arm. But although it broke my heart to see my grandpa like this, I wanted to be strong for him and prayed God would supply me with strength where there was lack of it.

What we talked about in that hospital room on that day was my grandpa's life. I had spent a lot of time with my grandpa before. When I was a little child I would sit on my grandpa's knees by his large desk and draw. Then later, when I was older I would talk to grandpa about my life plans, dreams and wishes. I liked to listen to his voice. He was the one to teach me how to type on a typing machine and encouraged me to write. He also heard me say I thought the unfinished painting of some Roma people and their cattle painted by his friend-artist in his room was ugly, just to realize later it was actually unusually beautiful. Grandpa would tell stories to my sister and me, but I had not heard much about my grandpa's life. And that day in the hospital we talked about it.

Grandpa came from a very poor family in which he was an only child and they lived in a small town. Grandpa was baptized and received his confirmation at a traditional conservative Protestant church. I still remember the black-and-white photo of him and his fellow believing friends from church. I was supposed to guess which one grandpa was and I could not recognize him. He was the tallest of all the boys.

After his studies in high school and early teaching experience, Grandpa studied Czech and history as a remote student at a university in Brno. As if he were telling me now... "When I was studying I would come home for the weekend to help out at home, and leave on Sunday with a loaf of sweet bread to last me for the whole week."

A moment that revealed some of his character was when he was taking his final university exams in the Czech language. He had been doing very well all the way through the oral part of the exam and the professor examining him was going to give him a high grade, when he suddenly asked if grandpa had read a particular book on Slavic history. Grandpa knew what it was about, but he had not read the book. Saying that he had not would mean a lower grade on his state exams. Saying that he had would mean a higher grade. What would he do? At that moment grandpa said honestly, he had not read it. What happened next was that the professor frowned and added, "In this case I cannot give you a high grade." And grandpa left the exam with a lower grade, but a clear conscience.

After the Second World War, the communists gained popularity and competed with other parties to finally take over the whole Czech political scene. Their movement appealed to many by offering people social justice and promising better conditions for workers, which were rather topical themes after the war. Although Grandpa liked the school and so-cial policy of the party and the proclaimed struggle for peace, his opinions did not correspond with the ideas of the party, as he said in his memoirs.

Grandpa spent two years in the military, met granny and started work-ing as a teacher in his hometown. As he was known for his responsibility and had a reputation of a skillful and renowned teacher, he was asked if he wanted to apply for a membership in the Party, which he refused several times as he did not want to engage in politics. When he thought about it later though, he decided to try it to be able to contribute to changes to the school and social policy. When he was accepted and his job as a secretary commenced, it dawned on him that he could not get off the train.

Aware that for going to church you could be penalized during the previ-ous regime, I asked grandpa what he did. He said that going to church and saying that one was a Christian would mean great persecution and danger to his family.

After the war, many people were so excited about the new system that many signed an agreement in which they gave up on their faith in order not to be fired. Teachers had to profess the ideology of communism only. Grandpa never signed it. Although their family did not go to church, his two sons were baptized after birth. My mom was born at the time when they could not have her baptized.

I tried to understand all the things as grandpa told me. I also tried to un-derstand the conditions under which he and his family had to live. You can hardly judge such things, and of who did what and why. I had no right to do that, and I did not. I knew life was difficult at that time.

I would always respect grandpa as a person who treated others with kind-ness, who had understanding for others, loved his family and wanted us to stick together. For this, who he was and so many other things, I treasured him so much.

That night in the hospital it was time to go home. I had wanted to encourage him somehow, so that he would not give up, and maybe I even said something like that. Even though I had wanted to pray with him and read the Bible, I didn't do that there.

It happened only when I was at home where I thought of him almost all the time. Later in the same year, grandpa went for another surgery. The doctor's verdict was not very positive. We still hoped it could improve, but at times we would lose any hope we possessed. Time mercilessly passed and we knew grandpa's state was worsening. They were talking about metastasis and increasing his morphine dosage.

I was worried about grandpa's physical state and his spiritual state. Where was he spiritually? Did he have peace with God like when he was young...? Or did he not...? Grandpa will leave soon and where will he go, I wondered. I hoped he was a Christian, but I was not sure. Grandpa had shown me his old Bible and a songbook before. I had told Dan about all this pain our family was bearing because of grandpa's poor state and he urged me to talk to grandpa and ask him if he believed in God and even pray with grandpa, and tell him I loved him.

I hesitated to do so. I thought it would be shocking to grandpa if I just came up to him and offered to pray for him. I knew if grandpa had any faith, he kept it deep in him as something very inner and private. And say to him I loved him? I understood why Dan was suggesting it, but I had never told grandpa. It would be my first time. I loved him so much, and thought that it was so clear, that I had not told him before. I do not know why but, however funny it may sound, I was also afraid that if grandpa gave his life to Jesus Christ, he would pass away right afterwards because the Lord would take him straight to Heaven. I did not want to lose my grandpa… But Dan told me again, that if grandpa did not believe I could lose grandpa forever, just by not talking to him about God. So I started seeking an opportunity when I could come to him.

And so one night, as our family was visiting our grandparents and attending to grandpa as he needed more medication, I stayed at my grandpa's bed after the rest of our family went to talk with granny in another room. I had been praying over this moment for such a long time and now it was there. Relying on God's strength, I forbade myself to cry or be too weak to do this. Suddenly grandpa and I were talking about faith. I do not remember what we said because it all seemed so fast. He told me he believed and I asked grandpa to pray with me the prayer of salvation, which was something like this:

> Heavenly Father, thank you for sending your Son Jesus to die for my sins. Please forgive me all the things I have done wrong in my life. I give my life to you. Accept me as your child. Jesus you are my Lord and Savior. Amen.

Afterwards I was relieved, both because my grandpa was saved by Jesus, and also that God had won the victory in me by asking grandpa to pray with me.

I purchased a Bible for grandpa and I tried to read to him from it every time I visited. His favorite passage was Psalm 23. *The Lord is my shepherd, I shall not be in want. He makes me lie down in green pastures, he leads me beside quiet waters, he restores my soul. He guides me in paths of righteousness for his name's sake. Even though I walk through the valley of the shadow of death, I will fear no evil, for you are with me; your rod and your staff, they comfort me. You prepare a table before me in the presence of my enemies. You anoint my head with oil; my cup overflows. Surely goodness and love will follow me all the days of my life, and I will dwell in the house of the Lord forever.*

My grandpa died within one month. It was one Sunday afternoon. I was working on some homework and heard my mom calling my name from downstairs. I immediately left my work and when I came down she was hurrying to pick up some documents and cried out, "Grandpa has died." All stopped in me. At that very moment something else also happened in me though - I received peace.

Later in my grandparents' apartment, I saw my grandpa's body and encountered other relatives who had come that day. If I had not had any hope for eternal life, I would have collapsed in despair that I was not going to see grandpa again. But it was different - I believed he had come from death to life.

We said goodbye to grandpa at two funerals - a civil one in our town, and another in his hometown where he had a short Christian ceremony in the cemetery. After the funeral in our town, I was talking to one relative of grandpa's who I knew was a Christian believer and who knew from my granny that I had prayed with grandpa. She thanked me for that. At the ceremony in his hometown, I was asked to read a passage from the Bible, grandpa's favorite Psalms 23, The Lord is my Shepherd. All of our family was there; and most were unbelievers. I was sad when we were burying grandpa, but I was also inexplicably peaceful in my heart because I trusted that all was well, he did not have to suffer anymore and I would see grandpa again, in Heaven.

By Dan

Jane had learned the very sad news that her grandpa, her mother's dad, had cancer and only a few months to live. This would be the first such loss in her life, and it would strike the family emotionally like the San Francisco earthquake. Jane's heart was quaking already, so soon after finding inner peace for the first time.

"Mr. Dan, grandpa must know God and Jesus and salvation first…before he dies. But I don't know what to do, what to say or where to start." That is a summation of the early part of our conversation. I listened better than I sometimes do because I didn't have a ready answer. I asked a couple more questions, and I prayed a very un-church like prayer. It was more of an SOS prayer for help. Then the answer came out of my mouth, "I think you begin by telling grandpa, 'I love you and I'm praying for you.'"

Jane firmly and immediately replied, "Oh I couldn't say that. If I told him that, he'd die immediately on the spot." Even then Jane knew some American idioms and they often surfaced at just the right moment… on the spot.

I was a bit stunned. I thought I'd given her a minimally invasive script, a simple and sincere expression of family love with an offer and promise of caring by praying. I'd learned earlier that it is generally true that there are few or no atheists in foxholes. Dozens of atheist students had told me in answer to my question that a family crisis, and dying could cause an atheist to pray. Only four had written "Nothing" would make an atheist pray, and my experience was that these four, even if they couldn't force some words of prayer, wouldn't reject someone else's offer to pray for them. Whenever an unbelieving friend confides a problem to me, I tell them "I will pray for you"…and I do. No one has ever replied, "Please don't pray for me, I don't want that, it offends me that you will pray for me." They always thank me, although I'm not sure if they thank me for praying, or if they thank me for caring enough to do what I do, when I care for a friend in distress.

"Jane," I replied, "If you can't say, 'I love you and I'm praying for you,' I have no more suggestions as to where you can begin." It was an awkward conclusion to this conversation. I don't recall if I said, "I'll be praying for you," but I do remember praying for her grandpa, and for Jane to receive wisdom as to how to approach him.

It wasn't until we began to write this book that I discovered how far off target I was, how much I misunderstood her reaction to my suggestion to say, "I love you and I'm praying for you." At the time of this conversation, I assumed the tension was her revealing her faith through a promise to pray. I thought that Jane meant that atheist grandpa would be so shocked that his atheist granddaughter is a praying believer that she feared he'd have a heart attack and die. That idea in my head was wide of the mark, a misreading of Czech culture, and carelessness with Czech history.

The issue was that it was not common for children to tell grandparents, "I love you." What is casually given out for free in American culture is often guarded and parceled out sparingly, or not at all, in the Czech culture.

In the USA, people can love anything and might carelessly say more than once a day that they love a particular sport, love a favorite food or restaurant, love a pet, love an entertainment artist, love a gift or holiday or a thousand other things. A child might talk on the phone with grandma, with the conversation concluding by the child saying, "I love you grandma, thanks for calling, goodbye." Then the child might turn to mother and ask, "Mom, can we have spaghetti for supper, you know I really love spaghetti." While this is 100% American, it is zero percent Czech.

In the Czech Republic, adults and students rarely use the word love in connection to movies, clothes style, or any of their favorite things. Love is an honored, protected and almost holy word.

Let's go deeper. Jane's grandpa lived his adult professional life during the communist era when parents seldom expressed any strongly held feelings or opinions to children, as it could put the family at risk. One especially didn't say aloud anything politically incorrect such as an unfavorable opinion of a political leader, or anything about faith such as "I'm praying for you." Schools had big ears with many spies; leaders that children liked and trusted, could ask questions and innocent children could repeat what they've heard, leading to difficulties for their parents. This reticence to express what one felt and believed became a generally practiced way of life.

So when Jane told me, "He'd die of shock," she meant that her words would be a breach of Czech cultural habits, especially for the generation that served in the latter half of the 20th century. One didn't speak so plainly of love or faith, and trying to hug someone was often met with a stiff back. One didn't do such things. Jane hadn't kept her faith a secret... grandpa already knew about this. But speaking to an older relative about the intimacies of love and prayer would be crossing a line that she imagined her grandpa couldn't handle.

Ten days later, Jane gave me an update on her grandpa's health and a conversation she'd had with him. God had given her the courage to tell grandpa, "I love you and I'm praying for you." I answered, or probably interrupted, by asking, "Is he alive or did he die on the spot?" Jane gave me a perplexed look as if wondering where that strange question came from; she'd forgotten what she told me she feared could happen if she confessed her love and spoke of praying.

"Oh no," Jane continued, "He told me 'thank you' repeatedly. He welcomed it as the greatest gift he could receive." It was a gift that kept on giving for weeks and months. What was never mentioned before became the anticipated dialog whenever grandpa and Jane were together. God's grace had melted a heart that seemed closed, but maybe was only choked by the system he grew up in and was waiting for such a day to blossom, as when his granddaughter made it safe for him to speak again of love and faith and God. One afternoon, these two held hands as grandpa met and welcomed God into his life so he could be with his loving Maker forever.

Jane had 'stepped into the waters and the waters divided' for her. That's an old idiom Christians knew and lived by a couple of generations ago. It comes from the biblical story of Joshua where we learn that Israel was told to cross the Jordan River, which seemed impossible since it was a hundred feet wide most of the year, and during the spring flood season it overflowed its banks and swelled up to a mile wide. But as soon as the Levites put their feet into the water, the river immediately stopped flowing twenty miles upstream. This was a miracle of God in response to the faith of the people. Today, irrigation siphons most of the water from the river, but at that time it was a foreboding river to try to cross with children and the elderly. It was when the believing leaders stepped into the river that the waters divided and opened to permit them to cross.

This was more than a one-time historical event; it became a lasting promise to you, me, and Jane. *"When you pass through the waters, I will be with you; And through the rivers, they shall not overflow you"* [Isaiah 43.2, NASB].

As soon as Jane said, "Grandpa, I love you and I'm praying for you," the cultural barriers divided and opened so she could walk through and into her grandpa's life in a manner culturally denied for half a century. The

Berlin Wall was not the only wall that needed to come down. That brick and mortar wall was a representation of the greater walls of fear and intimidation the system erected, to keep people from talking to each other about the most important issues of life. Jane had learned to trust God, not with a timidity that waited to see what God would do, but a courageous trusting that experienced God's help as she stepped into the water, or in this case, as she spoke to grandpa.

There are such cross-over moments when fear may paralyze us into thinking others will be so shocked by our story or conduct that we will be rejected and humiliated. But God has grace when we approach him to help us, and faith to provide for us. Faith will take us over, through, and beyond into a new freedom, with frequent confirmations of God's support. From the day Jane was given the courage to talk to grandpa, she has never again been silenced by fear.

The memory of her grandpa reminds me of other aging grandparents.

Nancy's dad and grandpa to our children hated God with a deep-seated resentment for most of his adult life due to a broken marriage. God received the blame for this. When Nancy welcomed Jesus into her life as an Ohio teen [at nearly the same age of Jane], her dad resented and rejected this and a tension grew between them. When Nancy went to a Christian college, her dad wouldn't take her to the train. And then Nancy did the worst of all...she married me, a pastor. Nancy and I prayed for her dad, Aaron, for years...three decades. At the age of 70, Aaron met a widow who'd moved into his neighborhood...a Christian lady. Mary was of the same age with a much-wrinkled face, but her face shined with an inner beauty of joy and peace that attracted Aaron. Nancy received a phone call one evening and after told me, "I just had the strangest experience. I think I talked with my dad but I didn't quite recognize him. The man I talked to wasn't angry or depressed, didn't complain or have a critical thing to say about anyone, and he didn't even stutter. He seemed at peace." For all the years I'd known him, stuttering interrupted every sentence as he searched for a way to complete a word. Days later, we learned that God used Mary with Nancy's dad, as He would later use Jane with her grandpa. Nancy's dad met and welcomed God and his Son Jesus, into his life, and he lived his later years with peace and joy...with Mary, as his wife.

My Reasoner grandparents, my mother's parents, were atheists, American style atheists with open hostility to Christians. My mother was a teenager during the years of the Great Depression and times were hard with banks foreclosing on many houses. Grandma Reasoner feared the bank would also take their home away from them, and bragged, "They'll never take me out of this house alive." She kept that promise. When the foreclosure letter came, the grandma I never met hung herself in the attic. Materialistic atheism was just empty bankrupt atheism when the material things of the world were taken away. My mother, age 17, was the one to discover the hanging body, and Mom learned the limitations of atheism to meet someone's inner needs when the pressures of life come.

My mom and dad became Christian believers when I was a few weeks old. It was a miracle transformation of a godless, churchless, hopeless couple, to a new life. My mother immediately began to pray for her dad, my widowed grandpa. She talked to him, of course, but he "wasn't buying" the religion thing. In his early seventies, he suddenly died of a heart attack. This was unexpected and it became the hardest spiritual crisis of my mother's life. She'd prayed for thirty years for grandpa and it seemed he died not meeting and trusting God.

After the funeral my Mom and Aunt Betty went to grandpa's home to pack up his clothes to give to a charity store. My mother picked up the Bible she'd given Him years before wondering what to do with it or whom should keep it. She happened to open the cover and noticed a recently added notation. Grandpa Reasoner had written an eloquent confession of faith in God and Jesus who had died for his sins and risen to give him life. He signed and dated it three weeks before the heart attack. God had answered her prayers.

So if you are praying for someone, it is always too early to become discouraged. And if you are running from God, and if someone is praying for you, it is likewise, too early to brag of your certain and lasting skepticism.

In northern Czech Republic, I asked a girl Jane's age about her two grandmas whom I had met and liked, but hadn't seen for two years. "How are your grandmas; are they enjoying life?" I asked. She looked at me as if this was a strange question and I should know better than to ask. "Of course they are not enjoying life. They are old and see life as something behind them with nothing to look forward to. Without God in their lives they just wait for it all to end forever."

I also remember a lady in Royal Center, Indiana. She was a grandma, and like Jane's grandfather, she was dying of cancer. I wondered how open and honest she was able to be with me, so I asked, "What do you think about when you are lying here in the hospital?" She confidently told me, "I think about when I might be going home." I still didn't know what she was thinking of...was she living in denial and hoping to be released to resume her normal life in a few days? "What do you mean you think about going home?" With a radiant smile she answered, "I think about when I'll go to my home above to be with Jesus and my Father God."

Jane's grandfather's expectation changed from a resigned, "It'll soon be over and I'll never be or know anyone again," to the anticipation of, "Soon I'll be cancer free in a new home in Heaven, thanks to Jesus."

∗　　∗　　∗

[Email excerpts from Jane]:

Dear Mr. Dan,

Today I was in the local hospital to visit my grandpa. Just imagine - he looked quite happy. When my mother, sister and I came into his room he was just talking to his roommate. He seemed very pleased. I think he is getting better. I ask God for it. Everything good, which happens to him, is from God. He shows him his mercy and love.

I think meanwhile that I am not brave enough to whisper to my grandpa that I pray for him. I am afraid of his reaction.

∗　　∗　　∗

Dear Mr. Dan,

When I think and talk about my poor grandpa I usually cannot help crying. I thought it would be good to tell you something about him for the case you would be interested but I did not know I would get so emotional. You asked me some more questions about my grandpa this afternoon but I was not able to answer. It is very difficult for me to manage to be involved in such a school pressure and the worries about my grandpa. I know that everyone has problems and worries and I do not want to bother you with them but I am trying to tell you and ask you not to be worried about me if you are worried. I believe that God will lift me up of this sorrow and worries...soon.

VII
The Applause Begins

By Jane

This would all happen in the last two years of my high school study. Soon after my grandpa died, I talked to my granny and that is when she told me she was praying for our whole family. I knew she was a Catholic believer as I had talked both to her and my grandpa when grandpa was sick. The three of us even read the Bible together.

I always liked talking to granny about it. She would often tell me that the most important thing about faith was to act accordingly; not the way she experienced it in her youth when people would bow down at church, but in real life they would gossip about others. Talks with my granny were always very encouraging to me.

Something was changing in our family. To me at that time, though, it appeared all the same. I was praying that my family could believe, but nothing was happening. My parents had always been wonderfully tolerant about my going to church, although they were quietly bothered by it. One thing which had changed, though, was that they no longer said they did not like it. It was as if they had coped with that. On Sundays, Dan or other friends would pick me up and we would go to church.

At that time I often imagined what it would be like if all my family could know Jesus and come to church. But it seemed so very impossible... I had times when I had faith that they would come to know him, but sometimes I would give up. Some of my believing friends stood bravely in this struggle with me and we just kept hoping God's light would shine even into their lives. But when was that going to be? Days and weeks went by and there was no significant change.

I sensed tension in the relationship between my mom and me. I felt there was a gap between us which I wanted to disappear. I think that the imaginary chasm was there not only because I was now a believer, but also because there were some things through which I had hurt her before when I still did not know God. I remember apologizing to my mom on two occasions for behaving badly and causing her pain in the years before I believed. It was not easy to say I was sorry, but I wanted mom to know I truly was, and that I wanted to be at peace with her.

Longing for my family to find faith in God, I looked for ways to minister to them. I tried to work hard at school and have good results. I would also leave pages from my Christian calendar on the kitchen desk for them to read every day if they were interested. The pages always contained a verse from the Scriptures and a short explanation. Sometimes dad asked me about something he had read, which made me happy as I saw he wanted to know more.

By that time I met four brothers who I liked to spend time with. Their names were Honza, Daniel, Tom and Libor. Honza and Daniel were at the first Camp and later I was introduced to the other two brothers. They were all fun to be with. Although they were from a believing family, they surprisingly did not believe in God. A friend of mine, Noemi, came up with an idea one day that we could go to a weekend Christian music festival with the brothers. There would be many bands, continual concerts on many stages, and also instructive seminars on music, art and life.

At the festival, which was my first Christian festival and my first festival ever, I talked to Honza one night. I still remember that hallway in the school where we were accommodated. We were eating our dinner; no one else was there because all the young people had gone for a program to the large hall. We, however, stayed behind and started a conversation about life. It is a very personal question but it came to mind to ask Honza why he did not believe in God. Quite directly, and to the point, "How do you feel about it Honza?" He told me that he did not feel like making that decision yet; that he might decide in a year or so, or maybe even later... "If you keep postponing that moment until later you might as well keep postponing it all the time until you finally never get to it..." The whole time I was shivering with excitement as the Lord had given me the opportunity to talk deeply about faith. I had never talked to any unbeliever like that.

Later that night, Honza told me that he had done it - he had talked to the Lord and decided to walk with him! I cannot express what great news that was to me. But this was not the only surprise that night. It was the last night of the festival and all the brothers and us girls were dancing and cheering in the first row, in front of the stage. That is when I heard another great piece of news - even Daniel had given his life to Jesus when he prayed in the prayer room at the festival. So these two brothers became my brothers in Christ on that very night!

The two brothers, Noemi and I comprised a group of young people meeting up to enjoy Christian fellowship together, pray, read the Bible, play games and have fun – our Youth Group in Moravská Třebová. The place where we met was a church hall of an old conservative Protestant church. The pastor was a very kind-hearted, older man who was happy we had that youth group, and supported and encouraged us. I liked that place so much. I did not know what it would be like when I went there the first time. I had never been to a youth group like that. But it was fine. There were only a few of us and it was a friendly environment. Our leader was a boy of our age, a student from the local military high school who tried to make the sessions attractive, interesting and accessible for us, and also for those who sometimes came to visit. Sometimes we would sing and play in the church together with the boys. You could talk about various things, life with God, and draw strength. I saw that as a Christian, one is not alone in this world.

One night our group was visiting a youth event in another church in Letovice. We had a nice time and later on that day we had a night of worship. Libor was singing next to me and I was praying for him. He turned to me after some time and asked me, "Could you go and pray with me please?" Libor wants to go pray! We found a quiet place in the building and he surrendered to God, asked forgiveness for his sins, and became a child of God. I remember it as if it were a week ago.

And what about the fourth brother, Tom? Even he knew the Lord. At the English Camp two years after my first Camp, Tom gave his life to Jesus. It was Pastor Daniel Smetana who told the team. But my family was still far from God. How long was it going to take until there was a change?

In our city, there was a little church station, which organized the English Club and also other programs for believers and unbelievers. I remember attending a series of lectures about the creation of the world with our whole family, and then a series about faith called, "The Case for Christ" according to a book by an American author. Throughout this program we watched The Gospel of John. It was in Czech but there was a possibility of discussion in English. As Dan invited all of us, I took my whole family there. At the final session, there was just my dad and I from our family. Dad enjoyed it and at the end of the session he talked to the visiting pastor. I knew the pastor was a very friendly Christian and found it amazing he had come all the way from Prague to our program. I knew him from the music festival and hoped he would answer my dad's questions. You can imagine how happy I was to see them both talking at the end of the session.

After that, my dad watched a DVD about Jesus, according to the Gospel of Luke. I was just watching TV. He came downstairs and said, "So I have watched the DVD." There was a prayer to accept Jesus at the end. I got excited, "And did you... pray the prayer at the end of the movie?" My excitement grew..."Yes, I did," my dad said. If he did, it meant he was now a believer! I think I just breathed out and said, "Wow... that is amazing..." My dad told me that he had actually always believed in God. He was baptized as a baby in the Catholic church as his parents were Catholics.

However, they did not go to church. (My ancestors were all Catholics except for my grandpa and his family.) Even though he might have believed in God before, on that day he prayed the prayer of salvation for the first time.

From that time on, we read the Bible together and prayed. How do you teach your own dad about God? I was placed into this position and had to persevere. We would get together every night before going to bed to read and pray. I had a bookmark which suggested the way to go through your Bible class: saying to the Holy Spirit you wish to be led by Him, then read, think about its meaning, and finally conclude the study and thank God for his Word for you.

With my dad and granny, I would go to church by car. Both of them liked it there and dad had many questions for our pastor who answered them patiently and diligently. One thing which dad liked to revise was K+M+B. What is it? It is a sign written on houses by volunteer charity boys, when people contribute to their cause at the beginning of the New Year. In Greek, *this means Christus mansionem benedicat: Christ bless this house*. And what is that symbol of fish which you sometimes see on cars and other things belonging to Christians? That was another thing that he liked to remind himself of. It is the Christian symbol of fish ICHTHYS - Jesus Christ God's Son Savior.

I continued attending lessons, which would prepare me for my baptism. On Easter, 2009, in my final year of high school, I would be baptized together with Daniel Marvan and another man! I prepared a testimony to tell the people attending, how I came to the Lord.

But I was also very nervous about the whole thing. I knew that only granny and dad were now believers, but my mom and sister were not. I imagined that it would be very unpleasant for them to come there and watch the whole ceremony. Apart from this worry, my baptism happened when I was going through another difficult period of bad thoughts. I thought about salvation, Jesus, and life in God. I was afraid I was not good enough for God and he could not have forgiven all the things I had done. I prayed that the thoughts would leave me, and said to God that I was his no matter what. However, I struggled with the thoughts even on the very day of my baptism until I was finally immersed in the cold water by Pastor Smetana. Afterwards I gave my testimony which declared 'no' to any attacks from the evil one, citing 2 Corinthians 5.17, *"Therefore, if anyone is in Christ, he is a new creation; old things have passed away; behold, all things have become new."* The reason why I had chosen this verse was also to help any unbelieving people, including my family, to understand that the Lord makes all things new and whoever becomes His child is made new.

I realized these spiritual attacks might have been meant by the evil one to confuse me and make me anxious so that I would feel insecure. God had actually equipped me with all the armor I needed, but I had forgotten to wear it. What is this armor of God? We can read about it in Ephesians. For free, every believer in Jesus, at the moment when they believe, is given the belt of truth, the breastplate of righteousness, something like "gospel shoes," the shield of faith, the helmet of salvation and the sword of the Spirit. As apostle Paul writes, with this armor the flaming arrows of evil will be put out. Without the armor, one can suffer a lot of wounds.

After God took my side and led me out of the bad thoughts, I was relieved. I hoped that the whole event of my baptism would serve as a testimony to my whole family, about what God can do in the life of everybody, who is willing to surrender to him. Would my mom and sister accept Jesus, though?

The second summer of English Camp, my sister went to Camp with me. She liked it a lot. The next year, together with my sister, even my parents decided to go to Camp, which I hoped would help them see the Christians I associated with were no sect, but normal people. It was after my parents' second Camp that my dad believed. But my sister came to her first Camp, second Camp, and third Camp, and she did not. But was she unchanged and untouched by God? We never know how he may be working in the lives of people, even some we've given up on long ago. After her third English Camp when our American friends, Connie and Dewey, who were part of the team, were staying in our house, I heard some whisper and I came to find out what it was. I came right when Connie was crying with joy over my sister's decision to follow Jesus! She did it!

Even my mom seemed to be more interested in God now. No, he had not forgotten about her. Our family would have a special time every night or afternoon when we prayed, read the Bible, and talked about what we should take out of it for our practical lives. We would take turns in reading, but I was the one to try to explain what it meant when our family did not understand. Sometimes they had a lot of questions. One day after we finished the Bible study, mom told us she now believed too. Mom believes! Again, I was almost speechless with awe.

This was something incredible. You pray for your whole family so that they could believe and then suddenly by the grace of God it really happens. Several friends encouraged us with the words from the Bible that salvation had come to our whole house [Luke 19.9]. I cannot describe my gratitude to God for allowing us to come to him and also taking the load from my back, and the worries I had about my family. Now all of them were Christians and that was so liberating.

But telling people about God is one thing and taking care of them and helping them in their life in him is another thing. Like we read in *Little Prince* by Exupery, "You become responsible for the thing you have bound to yourself forever." I felt responsible for our family, not because I bound them to myself, but because I introduced them to God, between whom and my family there was now a bond. They were new believers who were spiritual babies and needed to grow. What I tried to do was to read the Bible and pray with them every day, so that we would all stay in touch with God and not walk away from him again. Apart from our prayer time, we went to church together, talked to pastors, and prayed before meals. After some time, on my birthday, my family was baptized, which was the best birthday present I ever received.

It all happened so fast - only within three years; however, it might have seemed long during the whole time. In some families it takes a whole lifetime, and not even then, as some people's hearts are hard.

There was so much, which God had given me and I knew he was answering my friends' and my prayers for others. Believing granny, parents, sister, a group of believing friends, church... this was all a miracle!

By Dan

When is the concert finished? Is it when the last note has been played and the conductor lowers his arms to his side? The applause begins, people stand to their feet, even whistling as they clap, and in some cultures they shout "Bravo!" Only after the joy is expressed and released is the performance complete.

When is the football victory wrapped up and ended? Is it when the game clock ticks off the final second? For many it's not finished until the fans stop jumping up and down in victorious joy and the sports radio show finishes its reviews, takes its last caller and moves on to another sport or the next game.

When has the birth of the baby been fully accomplished? Is it with the first breath of the child and the separating of the umbilical cord? Many will agree that the birth is finished when it has been celebrated with photos, with cards, gifts and "Congratulations, what a perfectly beautiful child. We are so happy for you." The value of Facebook is that it provides an instant celebration vehicle as the photos go immediately from the birthday and graduation parties to our friends online.

Jane has been spiritually born and is experiencing God in ways that skeptics can't imagine.

What do you do with the highlights of your life...the team victories, the concert echoes, the Christmas pleasures, the vacation experiences? You talk about them. You celebrate by sharing these treasured mental pictures with family and friends who you hope will enter into your joy.

The applause praise instinct within Jane grows and she can't keep all the good news bottled up. It was natural for Jane to talk about the things she celebrated, and she had never before experienced anything so great as discovering the God who made her, knew her, thought about her with love, and had a purpose for her life.

So she talked. All of her believing friends celebrated with her. Some, who were looking for better cores to their own lives, smiled and were happy for Jane, even when they couldn't fully celebrate what she was joyful for.

And some couldn't celebrate at all. How can you celebrate with someone you think has made a terrible life decision, like going on life destroying drugs, or marrying someone you know to be a lying creep...or joining a phony religious sect?

One of the idioms English students learn is 'being caught between a rock and a hard place.'

What do you do when your heart sings and soars and you want your friends to enter this joy with you, but when you tell them they think you are "cuckoo?" You are between a rock and a hard place. You can't be silent because you've found the best thing in life and if your friends will listen they will discover it and celebrate too. So Jane began to tell others with a contagious enthusiasm.

She talked to grandpa and also to granny, and they welcomed her newly found faith as something of true value and soon joined in the celebration with their own lives of faith, beginning each day in the garden of their kitchen, reading and praying together.

Grandpa, who was soon to leave this world, who had known faith early in life and left it behind to live within the enforced atheist system, who for seventy years had weighed both faith and unbelief and found faith the more worthy and real, this respected granddad returned to faith in God and Christ, to finish his days on earth and to begin his eternity with the Father above.

After grandpa's departure from this world, granny continues to pray and find pleasure in God and Sunday morning worship events. Her aged countenance may be the most shining in the district. The applause grows and the celebration widens.

When the four brothers walk into a room the party begins. Jan, Daniel, Tomas and Libor are all close to the same age, with two of them twins. Since the twins are not identical, there are four distinct faces and personalities, each better than the other three. Like 'Rock, Paper, Scissors,' each triumphs the others at something. They complement each other like the four classic temperaments: sanguine, choleric, melancholic and phlegmatic.

Mom and dad had four hungry winners, hungry for the future and what it could bring, hungry to savor every second of life and adorn it with their own specialized zany zest, and sometimes just hungry. Feeding four healthy teenage boys must have been a challenge for mom, but a lot of fun for me at Pizza nights in our Svitavy flat.

We all became friends through English Clubs, English Camp, school classes and mutual friends. Jane's enthusiasm spilled over into the lives of these four as it did into many. It might be her full story that is heard or it might be a mention of how God had helped her this week.

These boys were now between that 'rock and a hard place.' The rock was the faith and prayers of their sincere believing and fully authentic parents and grandma. The hard place was being a teen student in an atheist school culture. They each resisted year after year becoming a believer, obediently going to church when forced, but refusing to let anything seep into their souls, or so they imagined. God heard the parental prayers and brought a couple of believing teen friends into their lives, one of them being Jane. One by one they turned from unbelief to join Jane in the joy of walking with Jesus. A Christian youth group was born so that none had to live a solitary faith. The applause is growing louder and wider, the celebration expands.

Jan and Daniel were the first to ask me if they could tell their stories at a post-English Camp retreat. They parked their chairs in front of the mixed group, boys and girls, Christians and atheists. They explained their decisions, their new faith, their recent experiences with God, and did it with sincere emotion and a clarity of logic that astounded me.

Judy Smith, an American who came to teach English at a camp remembers:

> "I'll never forget the summer of 2009. Tomas Marvan was in my English Camp group, and he added a lot of fun to our class time, as well as all week long during activities, games, evening programs, etc. One evening, toward the end of the week, after all of the planned activities for the day, I was walking up the hill from my cabin. As I came to the top, I saw Tomas talking to Czech Pastor Smetana at one of the tables. Tomas called out to me, "Judy, Judy, come here!!" So, of course I did. Tomas had the biggest smile as he told me he was now a believer; he had asked Jesus to forgive his sins and he wanted to follow him. Tears of joy formed in my eyes as I jumped up and down, excited, telling him how happy I was for him. Tomas and I gave each other a great big hug and he picked me up and swung me around and around, rejoicing together, along with the angels in heaven, in his "new birth." The next morning he wanted to tell all of us at our morning meeting that he was now a Christian. That was just the beginning!! Tomas has continued in his walk with Jesus, leading others, sharing his faith, and encouraging them to choose to follow Christ, too.

When will the applause end? It just continues to expand, and the volume grows louder and more enthusiastic. Daniel Marvan talked to a schoolmate and soon this young man became a believer and so alive in his heart. Like the circles widening from a rock tossed into a pond, the celebration expands.

At home dad hears Jane's applause over God's love and grace, and dad has questions revealing a real interest from his own heart. This fine medical doctor dad is peering into his daughter, trying to discern whether what she has found is good or bad for her, fake or real, to be commended or condemned. Mom and sister listen and watch, patiently enduring, wondering when it will meekly all end.

The Svitavy Core Team offers Lee Strobel's, *Case for Christ*, as a seminar in the town's cultural center. Mr. Strobel was an award winning atheist lawyer and journalist with the Chicago Tribune Newspaper. His research to defend his atheism to a Christian wife resulted in him becoming a convinced believer in God and the resurrection of Jesus. The *Case for Christ* book was available in Czech, but an accompanying DVD was only in English. Our team translated 3000 English subtitles and placed them back into the DVD at the correct locations. This was a major and worthy task.

One of the six seminar sessions discussed the miracles of Jesus. Were they fake or authentic? A discussion question was, "Which of the miracles impresses you the most?" Vladimir, Jane's father, replied, "The miracle that most impresses me is that when I read the Gospel of Luke I hear God speaking to me." Soon there would be a celebration for dad, with dad.

About this time student sister Eva told me, "I've seen many changes in my sister's life since she became a believer." As I held my breath for what would follow, Eva continued, "And I like every one of them." It was the Monday after an English Camp, and outside the door of our apartment building, that Eva told me she had prayed, confessed her sin and need, and welcomed God and Jesus into her life.

The applause for God's goodness and love grows louder, more and more are celebrating. School teacher mom, independently and confidently, brings fullness to the family joy as she also declares faith in Jesus. I will never again drive Jane to church on a Sunday morning...the family comes together, each face splendid with the peace and presence of God's Spirit.

It is time for Jane to be baptized, the baptism of a believer announcing to the world that "I'm a Christian now," announcing gratitude and obedience to God and Jesus. "Thank you for making me alive in the risen Christ. I will be what you want me to be; I'm your child and disciple to do, say, go and serve as you call me."

Her baptism words just before being immersed in water were "I appreciate that God speaks to us every day and encourages us; that he does not refuse anybody, but lovingly takes, bathes and clothes with new garments, and that there is the word of the Apostle Paul, that 'Whoever is in Christ, is a new creature. What is old has passed away, behold, a new life has begun'" [2 Cor. 5.17, Jane's paraphrase].

When Jesus was baptized, it was a newsworthy 'highlight reel' celebration moment. God the Father could not contain his joy, and he spoke aloud from heaven, "You are my Son and I love you; and you bring me great joy" [Mark 1.11, paraphrase].

The Father felt this joy also for Jane in her baptism...the celebration reached into heaven. This was the climactic moment of a season of celebration in Jane's life, but not the end of celebrations. The applause over a life in Christ continues. It is not Jane we are celebrating but the grace of God in her life, in the lives or her family and friends, then and now. Later, while baptizing her parents and sister, the resonant inner crescendo of awe for the spiritual life and beauty of Jesus in these, reached new heights. Please lift your hands and heart and join us in the applause and celebration of Jesus' living in those who are his.

VIII
Astonishing Encounters

By Jane

They were right when they said that high school would soon be over, however long it first seemed. Four years were gone and then it was time to say goodbye to all which I was used to - walking to school every morning, my classmates, teachers, our classroom, passing through the park by the school with tall trees, beautiful smelling flowers in the summer and icy pathways in the winter.

I was accepted for university in Pilsen, my dad's place of birth, and was going where he once used to live with his parents and two siblings. This large city was in the west of our country, an almost five-hour train ride from our town. I was very excited about my university study and the new location - what would it be like, this far-away place? What about the university, teachers, students?

Before I started studying there, I took a trip with Nancy Lupton to check out my new dorm home. It calmed me down and made me look forward, even more, to all that was ahead of me.

In my little bedroom, which I shared with a law student, there was almost no room for any item which didn't support our common studies, except my favorite picture, which I had purchased on a trip to America with my sister, to visit Dan, Nancy and other friends. It had a very powerful verse: *"I will guide you, I will turn dark places into light before you and make the rough places smooth,"* [Isaiah 42.16]. One of the rough places, for example, was our noisy dormitory, even though at first, I was happy enough about the new place that I managed to sleep without earplugs.

I liked my field of study and the way we had classes with my teachers and classmates. I soon found out that I was able to follow the lessons without any major problems. I felt at home with our faculty, in a very o d shabby building. As it was in the city center, I felt as if I was in the very center of all that was happening in the city.

When I went to my university, I received great support from my family and friends. They helped me with a variety of things. They also prayed for me and asked for updates as to what was going on in my life.

University days were quite routine, yet to my amazement, I saw that every day was different and had something very special to it. I would wake up with a lot of energy and courage to start a new day. One of the things I tried to do before I went to school every day was to ask God to have the day in his hands and use me in it if he wanted to. Again, like right after I had believed, when I was full of enthusiasm about God, he let me recognize his help every minute of my life.

That autumn was also very sunny. Usually it rains and is cloudy, but that first year it might have rained only twice before winter came. The beautiful sunny weather, and also something in the Pilsen culture, caused me to say that it was a peaceful city. I sometimes felt as if I had come back to a time when my dad lived there, as many historic buildings and means of transportation came from that era.

It is almost inexplicable, but whatever I did in Pilsen that year was what I sensed I should be doing. I was in the right place.

I met young people from a Christian group who I saw every week. We talked about our lives with God, sang songs and did sporting activities together. These people were a great encouragement to me and my new friends.

Once my cousin and I did sightseeing in the cathedral where we had a talk about faith. I knew that he would sometimes say he believed and sometimes he would argue that God could not exist, bringing up various reasons as to why he couldn't exist. I guess his problems were the dogmas which cannot be proven, such as, Jesus' birth from a virgin or his rising from the dead. What should we do about that? There is no scientific explanation for these miracles, as is the case of all miracles...we can only embrace them by faith.

On the very same afternoon when my cousin and I were leaving the church, there was a young boy by the door speaking Slovak. He told us he had been standing there the whole day without anything to eat or drink. I gave him my tea and he drank it all. He continued to share how he could not find a place to stay, that all the hostels were full and he could not afford a more expensive one since he was left only with $10. He asked us if we could call the phone numbers of the hostels on his list to help him find something. We did that because we were sorry for the poor boy, but there was no open place. The boy would have to stay on the street the whole night, which I did not wish to happen. I tried some phone numbers, and when one hostel told us they had some available places, my cousin took us there in his car. We felt badly for him as he was given a large room with about four beds and had to pay for each of them. However, he no longer had to stay on the street. After we left him in the hostel, we were walking back to our car and suddenly we saw him behind us. "Just going to buy some bread in the supermarket," he said cheerfully. When I came back home that weekend my mom told me she had heard a boy saying on the radio, that a girl and man had helped him in Pilsen and that he wanted to thank them this way. "Didn't that happen to be you?" mom asked.

On the streets of big cities, especially in the center, you can find a considerable number of homeless people. I was shocked at how many there were in the city. There was a girl who would beg for money, claiming she needed to buy a train ticket. She was a good-looking and friendly girl. I tried to give her at least some small money every time I saw her there. I was disappointed when my cousin told me she was a notorious drug addict. Once I managed to tell her I was not giving her money for drugs. She looked surprised and said she did not intend to buy anything like that. I was horrified when I saw her wandering about the square about two months later. She had put on weight and her face looked swollen and stained. It is hard to give money to homeless people, because some will not use it for food, but for things which may make a moment or two feel better. The results are devastating.

My talks with homeless people were mostly about them wanting money and me thinking whether I should contribute, or go on without giving them anything. I did not want to give them the money automatically without saying a word. I did not want to offer them only material support like money or food, but also the Gospel. But it was so hard… I always perceived it as a victory of the Holy Spirit in me when I managed to give them the money, saying "God bless you."

On the train you can meet many people; that would happen to me every time I went home for the weekend. One day I was travelling with my sister and there was a young student in our compartment. We exchanged a couple of words about our study and when we were getting off, I summoned all my courage and gave him a friendly tract, which read something like, "Have a nice day which God has made. Rejoice and be glad in it." What was his reaction? He looked at it surprised and I knew he was feeling uneasy. Maybe he just threw it away somewhere. Or did he think about the gift of one day?

On my way to Pilsen one Sunday afternoon, I was sitting in a compartment with two men, one of whom left early. The other man and I began to talk; he was very open and friendly. What I remember from the conversation are mostly fractured segments, but we talked about life and faith. He seemed to be interested in some eastern religions and our talk turned to the right way to live. Finally, he admitted he did not know what the right way was, even though he leaned towards "treating others the way we would like them to treat us." "But," I replied, "that is, if I am not mistaken, one of the biblical principles; that is what Jesus said…" *Give me your words, Lord.* "There are many different religions in the world, but only Jesus says about himself, '*I am the way, the truth and the life. No one comes to the Father except through me.*'" I do not know if the man accepted this truth, but when we were saying goodbye in Pilsen, he asked me to spread God's love and give it to other people.

Later I was at a job interview for one of the faculties, and soon after we started, in answer to one of the professor's question, I mentioned I liked to attend the Christian youth group in my free time. What followed was, "Are you a believer?" "Yes." The professor looked surprised. He told me he was not, and then he gave me the job.

Actually, at that time, I had an inner wish. I wanted to sing to God in a music band or a choir. I needed to find some people who sang in a Christian music group. This longing came surprisingly, because in high school I was not much into singing.

Then one day Dan came to see me in my new university city and I gave him a tour around the center. I also took him to the cathedral which is a true landmark in Pilsen. The cathedral welcomed us with its musty odor and cool air. As it was already getting dusk, there was not much light penetrating through the long tall windows. Everything was dark, but one sculpture hanging from the ceiling was lit – Jesus on the cross with people bowing down to him. I was fascinated by the whole scene before me. If I did not say it aloud to Dan, I thought it to myself and prayed… "Lord, I wish I could sing to you in this place at least once!" And he helped me fulfill my wish; I did not even have an idea when I was making the wish that I would sing there many times.

In those days, I liked to go to Catholic student masses near the cathedral. I was looking for a way to have a rest from the requirements of university life and all the busyness around me, and wanted to stay with God in silence.

Before Christmas I went to a mass and afterwards we decorated ginger-bread upstairs in the presbytery. There were some friends from school and I heard one friend say she was singing in a choir. I listened more carefully because that was what I was looking for and asked her for more details. She told me she sang in a choir which was not in Pilsen, but she referred me to a girl singing in the cathedral choir. This girl invited me to come to their next practice, which I did, and I liked the songs. Some of these were even from 19th century and older. They sang Mozart, Bach, Händel and others and I really enjoyed it!

The choir was not large in number – about 15 people altogether. I was a bit worried because I was not a Catholic and did not know if they were go-ing to be ok with that. In spite of my initial insecurity, the people accept-ed me warmly. There were even another two singers from a Protestant church.

I was happy that people from various churches in the city could help each other. There was a strong sense of collaboration between denominations that worked together and organized various events.

In the choir, the musical form was important, but did we sing only with our mouths? I believe we did not; I believe we also sang with our hearts...and that is what it should be about. This cooperation with Catholic believers encouraged and inspired me very much.

In the second year of study, my sister, some of the Marvan brothers, other friends, and I were part of an autumn youth Christian festival. It took place in our city, began on Friday, and continued until Sunday with the final service. The Svitavy Catholic Churches provided their church build-ings to the organizers of the festival, so that various events of the festival could be held in these facilities. On Saturday, we were part of a group of singers preparing songs with electric guitars and keyboard for the final service. I will never forget our singing both very old Czech songs for four vocal parts, but also new, almost rock songs with the church full of joyful people.

After this event, I got an idea. "Christmas is coming in two months, so why don't we organize an Advent concert? And wouldn't it be wonderful to hold it in the beautiful church where the fall festival was, Svitavy's red church?" I talked to my friends about it and they agreed. I also had to ask the director of the Catholic boys' choir if they would be willing to do something like that with us, and their answer was yes! When all of them agreed, we met in the church every Friday to practice. At the Christmas concert the boys' choir sang some of their songs; our high school and university group sang a medley of favorite songs, and we concluded by singing together a couple of old, Czech traditional Christmas carols. Our favorite song was a hymn coming from 15th century called "Let Us All Rejoice Together."

The most amazing thing about the whole event and preparations was that all of us from different Christian traditions could be together. At the beginning of every practice we prayed, however awkward it might have been at first, because some were mostly used to memorized prayers, while our musical group would pray from ours heads and hearts. But we overcame all of that and finally the concert night arrived, in which we sang together for God's glory, side by side.

I was still in the Pilsen cathedral choir, appreciating that I could sing at the services in the cathedral with them. But something started worrying me - I started thinking about the Lord's Supper or the Holy Communion and was sorry we could not receive it together. I also sensed disunity among us in how we behaved at church – the gestures like crossing themselves, bowing down and kneeling down was so different for me. There were times I was unhappy about it. Should I do that too? I wondered. Sometimes, especially at the beginning, I thought I should, but then I just did the way I saw it in my own church – just behaving naturally and doing what I was accustomed to.

When I started discovering the many differences, it caused me pain and I even started doubting whether I could overcome them and still believe Christians from various churches could collaborate and be in unity.

Finally, after some time, I accepted the following: in spite of the things, which are different in our churches, we still have one Father in Heaven. I perceive all denominations as people from one family – we are relatives, one coming from that place, having these customs, others coming from there, observing something else. All those who have accepted salvation in Jesus will be together one day.

While attending university, I did not go home very often. That was all the more reason I appreciated time spent with my family and granny. Granny had moved to a retirement home in the town where she had lived with grandpa and their children for many years. I looked forward to granny telling us wonderful stories about her life every time we visited her.

Granny grew up during the time of the First Republic and the Second World War. She lived in a country house with her parents and four sisters. They had a peaceful life but still there was room for a lot of adventures. One of the earliest memories granny mentions is that when she was a little child there was a car driving on the road by their house. She was so excited that she ran across the road to tell everybody and in her great speed, she did not manage to slow down and ended up with a brain concussion when her head banged the hard tiles of the large oven.

During the war, the area where granny went to school was divided into two parts. One day, granny, who lived in the Sudetenland, went to pick berries in a forest. She was stopped by the soldiers, the berries were spilt and she had to go home with nothing. Granny would be checked by the soldiers or run away from them in forests many other times afterwards. I cannot help smiling when I imagine my granny as a cute little girl running quickly from a soldier with a jar full of blueberries in her hand.

When granny was older it was time for her to go to her dancing lessons. She went to the first lesson, but when she was preparing to go to the next one, somebody called to tell the family that her father had died of a severe injury caused by a gate which fell on him that day. It was a tragic day and Granny mourned her beloved father for a long time. Like his whole family, her dad was a Catholic believer, but according to granny's words, he was looking for what he called the true faith.

Granny loved living on the family farm and when she looked over the many stripes of fields one day, how colorful they were, she decided to stay there her whole life. But a great love came and that changed everything:

One fall there was a village ball to celebrate the grape harvest where granny went and grandpa was there, too. They danced together but did not talk much. They had a good time but had to say goodbye. In January, granny received a note from grandpa, and instead of his signature there was a mark: Grape Harvest Festival...

Granny came there and danced with grandpa...and it did not finish with just that one dance. "Then we danced together for another sixty-two years," as granny likes to conclude her story. I cherish those moments when granny narrates what happened to her and her family when she was younger, and I like to add things from the stories when granny tells them and forgets about some details. Granny is a light to everybody around her. And my mom and granny are so similar in many things.

To season this story about granny, let me mention that granny also sometimes tells my sister and me how faithful she was to grandpa. "Although I had seven surgical procedures on my body and went to a medical spa after every one of them, I was not interested in a single one of the men around me. They might have asked me out to drink coffee with them or go for a walk; I would always thank them and go my way." One friend once asked granny with a surprised expression, "And you really had only that one man?" (The friend had more.) Granny answered, "Yes, I had only one. I loved him and I loved him all my life."

I have always sensed peace and harmony in the relationship of my parents and grandparents. No matter what they went through, they endured together. There were some invisible ties. Their relationship of love, mutual understanding, patience, helpfulness and security is not a matter of course, though. When I imagined mom and granny, who did not have to have any other men because they had their husbands, I thought of some people changing partners very often. I was shocked to overhear a conversation between a girl and a boy going to lunch after school. "They have split up. They went out just for a few weeks and are not together anymore." I heard, "But it happens very often. They go out, sleep together, and that is the end of their relationship." How can we know that this behavior is right or not right? I looked for such an answer, which God gives me. *"But because there is so much immorality, every man should have his own wife, and every woman should have her own husband"* [1 Corinthians 7.2]. To be faithful to one's own husband. To be faithful to one's own wife.

And then there is another option. Some people will decide to serve the Lord all their lives without getting married. God has prepared something unique for each of us.

By Dan

It was Good Friday and I was ill, and this was the one weekend that illness could not be permitted in my body. But there it was. Bronchitis, probable pneumonia, fever and cough with aches and pains. I took many cold pills plus aspirin, ibuprofen or Tylenol, rotating the use of these pain and fever reducers. With these partial remedies I went to the 5 p.m. church service that honored the crucifixion of our Savior. While going to church was a physical ordeal, it was only the beginning of my evening. At 6:30 p.m. I needed to drive three and a half hours to Prague to pick up our guest John Stewart.

John Stewart is a British author and illustrator of children's books, which have a Christian moral and finish with a Bible verse. John is a lifetime artist and his illustrated books are masterful, while his story telling skills match or exceed his writing skills. Children adore him and flock to him and don't wish him to leave…one more story please. Teachers of children and school administrators feel the same way, and I knew that in his heart John was an evangelist. We booked John into a full schedule of schools, clubs, library, and church events.

John would live with Nancy and I in our flat and I must first drive to meet and receive him at the airport and then make the return trip. I knew I was too ill to manage this no matter how heroic I felt, and I didn't feel anything but a longing for a bed. Josef, a high school English teacher, friend and brother in our shared faith, volunteered to do the driving. He was my hero this night.

Jane recognized what was happening and pulled me aside to provide words of encouragement. "Mr. Dan, I have prayed for you and I believe that soon all will be fine."

Jane always has faith and usually discernment of what God is doing and what must be done. Her words were an encouragement with hope that God would fulfill his plans for the coming fortnight. But while welcoming her prayers, I still felt one hundred percent ill.

With a liter of water, aspirin and cold meds, I slipped into the passenger seat, Joe into the driver's seat and we were on our way to the Prague Airport to welcome John Stewart. I prayed that neither John Stewart nor Joe Dvořák would catch what I was carrying.

The journey was long; Joe's company was a gift; and my company was somehow tolerable. The plane was due at 10 p.m. and we pulled into the airport parking area at that time. I painfully stretched and pulled myself out of the blue Czech Skoda Fabia automobile. We were a few minutes late and John might be standing in the Terminal One hallway feeling deserted. Joe and I walked slowly toward the door where one expected to meet arriving passengers, and I hoped I didn't stagger too much and that I could somehow mask how ill I was.

John Stewart's plane was late in arriving and delayed twenty more minutes. Twenty minutes isn't so long I thought, as I kept my eyes on the large board announcing the arrival or delay of planes.

Suddenly, and unexpectedly I noticed something...I turned to Joe standing next to me, "Hey Joe, guess what?" He looked at me a bit confused and asked, "What?" "I feel great," I said. Joe looked at me a bit bewildered and not comprehending. "Joe, I've been so ill I didn't know if I could survive the trip or would end up in a hospital emergency room. But I feel perfectly well. I've been healed...completely...never felt better. Jane prayed and somehow had the assurance from our Lord that something like this would happen. God answered her prayers!"

Ten minutes later, John Stewart stepped out from the customs inspection with his luggage and we were on our way to serve in Svitavy, the Czech Republic, with the knowledge that God had everything in control. I celebrated all the way on the two and a half hour return trip, which was faster with little traffic at that time of night. John's two weeks of service in Svitavy was special. We had him in front of children, teens, adults, and he winsomely drew all to himself and his Savior. God indeed had won a full victory. While this sounds dramatic, and for me the healing was akin to a surprise party, answers to prayer are not unusual with newer Czech believers.

When Czech students put their faith in Jesus, the parental response is varied. Jane received permission to be the friends of the Lupton's and to attend a Sunday church service. But another teen met with fury from his parents. "You can never go to church, never go to the English Club, never go to English Camp, and give me that Bible; we don't want that book in our home." A not yet believing high school student, yet a curious watcher and seeker, told me that at one time she was invited to a Christian rock concert. When her mom asked where she was headed to, this teen answered, "to a pub to drink with my friends." I don't advise or condone this deceit, but the teen knew that going to a village pub to drink and come home drunk was okay with the parents, but going to a Christian concert would be forbidden and stir undesired wrath.

So, how do teens, recently reborn spiritually by faith in the Savior, grow to strength and maturity in their walk with Jesus, and what experiences do they have? When parents react with fury and grounding and a set of anti-faith laws, opportunities become limited. I've not yet known of a parent taking away a student's computer, so the Bible can be found online, and one can receive mentoring and friendship through Facebook and email.

The one thing no parent has ever been able to deny is the liberty of a teen talking to the Father above in prayer. When educational growth opportunities are hindered, prayer opportunities may be enhanced. *"He shall call upon me, and I will answer him; I will be with him in trouble"* [Psalm 91.15, NKJV]. Jesus invites both Czech and other new children in his family, *"Ask, and you will receive, that your joy may be full"* [John 16.24, NKJV].

Frequently, in the Czech Republic and the USA, friends ask me to pray for them. I agree to intercede for them, and I do. But I've often also suggested, "You might wish to ask one of our newer Czech believers to pray for you. God always answers their prayers." As a hungry baby cries for milk and miraculously mom always feeds him, so God hears the cries of his new children, and maybe especially those who have turned from atheism to trust him. I've seen a dying infant healed, hatred turn to love, and recently a prayer answered before it was spoken.

This brought some confusion to the Czech university student, even when I explained, "God does this sometimes, even promised to sometimes answer our prayers before we ask. *'I will answer them before they even call to me. While they are still talking about their needs, I will go ahead and answer their prayers'*" [Isaiah 65.24, NLT]*!* The question came back, "Why should we pray if God knows our needs and may even answer before we ask?"

I explained, "Well, for one thing, that is the purpose of life...to know and enjoy God and have a relationship with him. Adam and Eve had a daily meeting with God in the Garden of Eden before they sinned, which meant they talked with God when they didn't need anything and had nothing to ask for. Can you imagine meeting with God only to enjoy him and not to ask for things? To be near him, thank him, and feel his love?" And as to Isaiah's words, he still says the person prayed. God may answer before we pray but not necessarily without us praying.

Jane and our Czech believers know about prayer. About the time Jane left for university, one in our group had a difficult relationship end and this wounded his faith and he became depressed. We were all concerned about this brother whom we loved. Jane and her friends organized a prayer vigil named "PUSH." Although they are all Czech, the acronym is English. PUSH = Pray Until Something Happens. On a seven-day cycle, two people agreed to pray for this friend on their appointed day of the week. This friend and brother who was prayed for by the PUSH team is now fully restored, mentoring others and a partner in English Camps and music ministries. PUSH has been going strong for five years. Even now as you read, there are Czech PUSHers seeking God's intervention grace for one or more.

I would miss Jane as she went to a university five hours away in Pilsen, the beer capital of the Czech Republic, of Europe and even of the USA. "True Pilsner flavor" means "as good as the best beer in the Czech Republic." But Pilsen is more than a beer city, it is a multiple university city and Jane's adventures with God would increase, if such is possible.

As you have discovered, Jane is gifted in talking to people one to one, although she is reluctant to admit it. When Jane walks into any room, she assumes everyone there is a friend, and soon they are friends if they weren't before. She thinks she is shy and doesn't easily talk to strangers, yet she is what Titus 1.8 calls a *lover of strangers.* She delights in talking to people and letting Jesus guide the conversation. So God sends strangers to her.

Jane sent me an email one Monday, telling of her five-hour return to Pilsen from a weekend home in Svitavy. On the train a man noticed some Christian book or magazine Jane was reading, and he made some disrespectful comment about this. Americans can easily imagine this happening in the USA, but they have no idea how culturally rare this is in the Czech Republic. The only people who talk on trains are drunks. All others sleep, read their books, listen to their MP3 players or stare out the window watching the mountains, castles, and poppy seed fields pass by. No one talks to strangers. Jane gave a gentle and positive reply, affirming her faith, but not revealing a hint of offense received, because with Jane, no offense was taken. That opened up a two-hour conversation with Jane telling her story of atheism to faith and a walk with God.

Another time a stranger startled her by asking, "Are you a Christian believer?" Jane replied, "Yes, I am a Christian believer." For two hours Jane answered his questions and told her own story. This night, there was one seeker of God and truth, in Pilsen. The Lord knew the best-prepared person to send him to. The convergence of their paths was in God's timing.

As Jane moved to the university in Pilsen, the English Club ministry and service in Svitavy was reaching its peak. We led a student English Club and a second and separate adult English Club in Svitavy, plus a student English Club in Moravská Třebová, over the mountain and through the tunnel southeast of Svitavy.

Jane had been at the first English Club meeting in the Ottendorfer Building better known as the Red Library. First as an unbeliever and later as a believer, she became a student anchor who rarely missed any club event. English Clubs were not church type meetings; they were friendship clubs, helpful and fun times that built bridges between believers and non-believers. Jane knew we would feel her loss, and she also would miss these clubs that had been a part of her life from the beginning of our friendship. Jane thought and prayed about what she should do. She knew she must come home occasionally to see her sister, parents and granny. So for her first two or three university years, she arranged her schedule to take the five-hour train from Pilsen to us twice a month, to serve in the English Clubs.

I would send her via email the activities or games she would lead, or a song to teach. She always came prepared and experienced much joy in serving her own community, even while studying at the far end of the country near the German border to the west.

I'm a bit embarrassed, yet full of satisfaction as I recall the schedule. The slight embarrassment was that the train arrived at 6 p.m. and our clubs began at 6 p.m. Jane would rush from the depot to the club, and her beloved parents must wait until after the club was finished to greet their first born daughter.

Jane had once dreamed of being a ballet dancer, and dance is a partner to music. We knew Jane had a fine voice and she was now having fun discovering that she could sing. She joined the English Camp band as a vocalist and her voice could both sing and lead others in singing in a bright and pleasing way.

In her university city, Jane began to sing more widely including the Cathedral choir. In Svitavy, she would sing as vocal leader in our church worship group, and several English campers formed a band with guitars, keyboard and vocalists. It was actually the English Camp band continuing during the other 50 weeks, in churches and a variety of venues.

Svitavy doesn't have a cathedral, but it has a large Catholic church known as the Red Church to distinguish it from another Catholic church known as the White Church. A concert was arranged during the Christmas season for this English Camp band and a boy's group within the Catholic church. The outside temperature was minus one Celsius or thirty degrees Fahrenheit, and the inside temperature was exactly the same. Catholic cathedrals and churches are rarely heated in the winter. You can watch this band sing, "Oh Happy Day" in a Christmas concert with Jane singing lead. You'll find it in YouTube using these key words: "Svitavy English Camp Oh Happy Day." You'll notice the coldness of the room as the breath of each singer can be clearly seen, but also notice the warmth of God's mercy in the souls of the singers.

You may find it curious the way in which Catholics and Protestants see each other as friends and often as brothers and sisters, even to serving together, as in this concert, charity events and prayer meetings for the community. But those who have read stories of the persecution of Christians during the communist era will better understand it. One of my heroes is Richard Wurmbrand who spent 14 years in horrific prisons in Romania. When you read his books you will notice that in communist prisons those prior to prison were Baptists, Lutherans, Catholics, Brethren, Adventists and more; inside, were one in Christ. That is because prison could be avoided by denying faith or hiding one's faith. Only those whose faith in Jesus was so strong it couldn't be hidden or denied were sent to prisons. In this way, social Christians, pretend Christians, holiday Christians, and skeptical Christians were soon eliminated as they chose the politically correct path of agreeing to become atheists. What remained was a purified by fire group of believers, who loved God, prayed, suffered together and encouraged each other, while the label of the group they associated with had lessened value. Anyone in Eastern Europe over the age of 30 was raised with these realities and memories, and they linger on.

A small Orthodox group was building a chapel a few years ago, and they are still building it today. The Orthodox Priest is a layman and part time priest and a friend of mine. I went to see the progress on their building three years ago, only to discover some seemingly insurmountable problems. I offered, "Let me pray for you and this problem...now." We stood in a prayer circle as I prayed. Within 36 hours the problem was solved and for the next two years, whenever I saw my Orthodox friend, he thanked me for that day of prayer.

Our partners and friends in the northern portion of the Czech highlands, some 40 minutes from us, are the Baptists. How I rejoice in every opportunity to be with them, as our hearts are one in bringing more to the Savior and helping young believers grow strong. We have often used their church building and two cottages, not as renters, but freely with their youth participating, knowing we are all in one great extended living family of faith.

A Catholic teacher in a public high school sees herself with me as missionary partners bringing Jesus to students, and she is right. When you live in a sea of atheism, praying believers in Christ are your friends. We know we are 'salad' friends and not blended friends; the distinctions clearly remain, even as we like and respect each other.

And I pray for the other kind of friendships for Jane and many young believers. The believers are strong and real in their walk with God, but they are scattered far and wide across the nation, and it isn't easy for them to meet each other. Their future spiritual health requires marriage partners who love and follow Jesus with them.

The Czech Republic is in many ways a gentle nation. Even the overthrow of communism is remembered as the Velvet Revolution because it was accomplished through street demonstrations, but without bloodshed. But atheism has turned the youth of the nation to an amoral society and a world leader in pornography. God has led Jane and our many other newer believers to make this an area of repentance and resolve, that by God's grace they shall live as friends with those in the world, yet live as children of God keeping their bodies and souls clean for the Savior's use, and in preparation for marriage and life to come, until Jesus' return.

IX
Taste and See

By Jane

"Shen, Shen!" little Ann called my name, meaning "Jane," and then, even louder she cried out, "Look!" The tiny little girl of about five years of age swiftly climbed an armchair and jumped off. Then she climbed it again and jumped off as before, expecting my reaction. What a cute little sweetheart, I thought to myself. "Annie, good jooob! Veery beautiful!" I knelt down to her and lifted her up. She was so light that I would often take her to my arms. In every picture I took with her, Ann grinned from ear to ear, showing all her teeth. This child definitely had one of the biggest smiles of all the children at the Children's Home, who I liked to call angels, 'malaika's' in Swahili.

There were about eighty children altogether, from very young ones of pre-school age to high schoolers of about age eighteen. Some were enthusiastic and more talkative, some were shy and reserved. Every child had their own story of what happened to them before they started living in the Home. They came from various parts of the country, mostly the west of Kenya, and Nairobi. Their families were often broken with both of their parents dead or seriously ill. In cases when the children had extended families, they often could not be taken care of by them, for financial reasons. Some saw their mothers being raped and then slaughtered in the cruelest of ways, or their fathers and siblings tortured and beheaded, as a result of the post-election violence about a year before. The children had been brought to the Home by their guardians responsible for them. Some had been living there for five years; others came when I had stayed there for some time and were our new children.

I came to be a volunteer at First Love Children's Home in Kenya, after a series of events in my life that made me think and make a decision. I believe God started preparing me for this stay even through things that were not very pleasant.

"Lord, I have asked you so many times to take this thing away from me and I still have it, there is no change. When it finally seems to have left me, it appears later as before. Can I possibly live without it?" I was praying and it was a desperate prayer. The chronic tonsillitis I had was at its worst again and there was nothing I could do about it. I had had it since I was nine and was about twenty now. Sometimes I had nothing strange in my throat, only to find out a week or so later, the throat was a mess again. I felt I had tried out various medicines, classic and alternative, changed my lifestyle and eaten more healthy food, but it did not bring the desired effect.

In my second year of university, the illness was getting worse again and it came to mind that I might try coming back to my specialist to consult him, maybe for the sixth time in all those years. I remember making the appointment and crying over the whole situation after a youth group meeting in Pilsen, where a believing friend comforted me and promised she would pray for me. I told her that I perceived talking to the doctor as the last chance to get better, and was afraid of what I'd hear. After talking to my friend, though, I felt more confident and laid it all into the Lord's hands.

The day of my appointment came. I told the doctor about my long-term problem and he asked me to come in a week, saying he might see more then. I prayed even harder afterwards and asked God to guide the doctor and me, so that we would come up with an idea as to how to fight it completely. I was actually very much hoping he would suggest surgery to me. That day I came to his office full of expectations. After he checked my throat, he found out the same problem as in the previous years. For a moment we did not speak. I was waiting for his verdict when I got an idea. I shook my fear off me and asked, "And do you think that surgery would solve this problem?" "Well... that is for sure," he said decisively. In a short moment, the doctor was already typing a request for my hospitalization! Until the very day of the procedure, I did not stop thanking God for the option of surgery which I believed he could use to completely rid me of my illness.

I must have been the happiest patient in the whole hospital. The surgery was performed under local anesthesia, so I paid attention to all that was happening. Even afterwards, when I was pushed to my bed in a wheel-chair with bloodstained tissues, I sensed the Lord's presence and felt only joy. He was simply in everything with me. How grateful I was when lying in bed and I realized what he had done for me... "God, you saved me spiritually, giving your Son Jesus to die for me at the cross, and now even physically, so that I do not have to suffer from this illness. For this I would love to do something for you. Anything I can. For this deliverance you have granted me, I want to live for you even more. I will go anywhere for you."

I wanted God to send me somewhere I was needed and could serve. I had not even finished the prayer, when Africa came to mind. It appeared all of a sudden and made me think of missionaries and other workers there, not always in comfortable conditions, giving their lives to save lives, please souls in distress and help them carry their burdens. "Even to Africa, any-where. Send me and I will go." I also told God I wanted to give him one year of my life, full-time. But when I gave it more thought and realized that I was now without the chains of the illness, I changed my mind. "Not only one year, but for this great mercy I want to give you all my life, even more than I did when I started believing in you." The desire to go somewhere I could serve full-time, though, remained in me.

A few days after the hospital procedure I returned home, my throat got better very soon and I have not had any problems like those ever since. But what about my plan to go and serve? One year passed without any-thing happening. I would think of my promise to God but I did not do much about it. When I heard someone mentioning something about mis-sions, I asked them for more information, but otherwise I did not look for it myself. I somehow thought I would not succeed in finding anything and was hoping something would appear by itself out of the blue. It was almost two years after I asked God to send me somewhere, that he started answering my prayer and broke my passivity.

A friend of mine from Great Britain came to our church one morning and we started talking about missions and Africa. I confided in him that I would like to go on a voluntary trip to serve and he told me about an American lady who went there once in a while and suggested I could join her. He promised to send me her contact and I was very excited. But one month passed, even another one and I did not hear from him or the lady. Finally I gave up and was where I had been before. Some time passed and then I decided to tell Dan. I knew he was part of a Christian organization called, First Love International, and wondered whether he might know of some opportunity to serve overseas. It took us some time to finally contact Tom Clinton, First Love Director, and he had a great option for me. "Jane, you could teach English at a language school in the Philippines." When I read his email it all seemed so hopeful but then again, it did not seem to work. "Do you have a degree in teaching English?" "I do not," I had to admit, which meant that the job was not for me. I was disappointed, but not for long. "There is one more option. There is an orphanage our organization has in Kenya. Would you mind going there?" "I would love to go!" When Tom suggested it and mentioned Africa, I knew this was "Africa" again - as in the hospital! Way to go!

But Africa...there is danger, there are illnesses, I can get infected, and the accommodation will probably be under bad conditions; my parents were worried about me. But there was someone who explained to us that the Children's Home is in a safe location, that there is running water from the well and that the accommodation is luxurious compared to most of Africa. This person was Dan. He talked to us about all the necessary things, my parents agreed, and my preparations for the stay could start. I needed to raise funds, which I first knew nothing about. How do you collect money for your stay? Dan knew how to go about it though. This faithful brother in Christ and dear friend with a servant's heart did me a great service by visiting churches he knew and preached there, talking about the mission and me. I will never forget about his updates on how the raising of funds went. Every month, from February to May there were more and more people who contributed to my stay in the Children's Home. Thanks to Dan's great help, these donors from far-away American churches and my home churches in Litomyšl and Svitavy, we raised an amount large enough for me to afford to go there. When I look back on these brothers and sisters' support I realize how grateful I am to God for all, even now. And that is how I came to arrive at First Love's Children's Home one rainy night that September, to be welcomed by the children and the house parents, who had prepared a warm meal for me.

What an extraordinary experience it was to meet all the children. One by one I started remembering their names. I also started getting used to the new schedule. I soon discovered that the children's daily program was very busy. On weekdays, they got up at about five or some even earlier, did their homework if they did not manage it on the previous night, had breakfast and were driven to school by bus, so that they would be there at seven when school started. After lunch, they still had classes until half past four, arriving back home at five. What followed was polishing of shoes, washing their clothes, and evening devotions (small church services), before dinner at seven. Following dinner, the children did their homework and were ready to go to bed after nine.

Very soon after my arrival, I started a volunteer service, which was on the list of things Tom suggested I could do there - teaching at the local primary school. I taught English classes and Creative Art that included painting, drawing and music. A teacher, when introducing me to the children said, "God has given us a new teacher. Her name is Jane and she is a very good teacher." I was wondering whether I was or was not a good teacher, as this was going to be my first long-term practice, but these flattering words encouraged me. The lessons at the school turned out to be very relaxed and children participated in them with enthusiasm. Sometimes their enthusiasm seemed to go beyond any boundaries, and I had difficulty calming them down. Never was it too overwhelming, though. The school children liked to shake my hand to welcome me or say good-bye, and tried to jump up so that they could touch my hair as "msungu's" - white person's hair is so different.

Back in the Children's Home, when the children were running around looking for Barbie dolls and toys they could play with, climbing on me, drawing on sheets of paper in crayon or colored pencil, I recalled my sister's and my childhood and the way our mom would let us play while she was sewing in our little kitchen. I tried to follow her example in creating a warm and loving environment so that we would feel happy and secure. The children and I also had a new club for their free time called the Art Course. In this Saturday course, we learned how to paint and draw, using all possible kinds of techniques. Not having studied fine art, I often remembered what we did in our art course when I was a child. Among our teachers, there was a young lady with whom we would paint mostly angels and people, copying paintings by famous artists and learning from them. With her sweet spirit, this teacher who wanted to become a nun but finally decided to marry, left a wonderful mark in my heart. I also liked to recall some other art teachers who used to teach us art and from whom I drew inspiration for my art classes.

In the dining hall, Tom wished a big ship full of animals curiously looking out of Noah's Ark, to be painted on the wall. But what would you have done if the children had come up to you afterwards and said, "These walls are still so empty. We want some flowers, trees, animals...?" I thought about it and had the idea to paint the Garden of Eden.

One of the things I also did with the children was to teach them how to play the guitar. The truth was that the year before, I still had not learned how to play it! A Catalonian lady had taught me how to play three screechy basic chords, but besides that I knew nothing. Three months before I went to Kenya, I promised myself that I would practice playing every single day of June and see if I could improve even without a teacher. At first I was discouraged, because I did not seem to improve; the guitar kept moaning and giving out tones which pleased no ear, until one day it sounded the way I had heard it from my friends – guitar players.

When I came to the Home, believe it or not, I was already able to play the basic songs, and once they suggested I could help lead the evening devotions, I looked up other songs so that, in total, we learned about thirty altogether. When I look back to June, I could not even dare to imagine playing there with the children, as my playing was very clumsy and slow, but the children were patient with me and guitar music became popular in the Home.

I was especially proud of about five children who learned a few chords. One boy, Isaac, mastered playing so well, that he played at the devotions with me for the whole last quarter of my time there. Somebody told me they were not sure if he was a believer and I hoped that God would touch him through the music he played. It was Isaac, who later asked me to lead their Music Club at school, which was one of the Friday afternoon clubs children went to before the weekend started. With no special education in music, I hesitated, but then decided to join in and have fun with the students. Our clubs turned out to be so crowded that we could hardly fit everyone in the room. We sang English worship songs together with the guitar and sometimes had singing contests. I saw God's help all the way through and was happy about the students' excitement.

Our headmaster was a very enterprising gentleman who wished to develop the children's potential as much as possible. He suggested to me that besides teaching some music theory to the children, I could paint some pictures in the old assembly hall that had been reconstructed and painted by First Love workers, and now looked amazingly clean and beautiful. He wished for some quotations or verses, spiritual or academic, to be displayed. I prayed about this a lot as the responsibility was on me, and I was aware the painting would be there for a long time. I thought, "It needs something timeless and Bible verses are like that, aren't they?"

When choosing phrases, I remembered the Muslim students who did not believe in Jesus as the Lord and Savior, and was sorry for them. The verses I wrote there and hoped would help them were: *"I am the way, the truth and the life,"* says Jesus [John 14.6]. And, *"Salvation is in no one else but Jesus"* [Acts 4.12]. There were other Christian verses, but these I thought, spoke clearly about Jesus' sovereignty.

One Muslim student especially touched my heart and I prayed for him. What a surprise it was for me to be greeted by him on my last teaching day. "Bye, Teacher." - "Ahmed...! God bless you."

Although the work in the school was sometimes stressful for me, I appreciated I could do it. I admired the teachers who taught there every day and spent so much time with the children. They taught daily with no central heating in the classrooms and no running water in the whole school; the broken windows and damaged ceilings were no exceptions. In windy weather, there was a lot of dust coming from the soccer field behind the school. Obviously, the school was in need of reconstruction, but in spite of the hard conditions, there was a friendly atmosphere. I will never forget drinking tea with the teachers every morning at eleven. "Are you a believer in Jesus Christ?" or "Are you born again?" were only some of the questions they would ask. "Trust him more, place all your worry on him, surrender to him," a colleague encouraged me one morning.

How similar to this advice, was the verse of our children's program in the Kibera slum earlier that year. *"Trust in the Lord with all your heart and lean not on your own understanding. In all your ways acknowledge him and he will make your paths straight"* [Proverbs 3.5,6]. There must have been more than one hundred children participating that week. We played games together, made crafts, learned new practical and educational things, and spoke together practicing English. Some of their names have remained in my mind… Joseph, Mary, Peter, Natalie, Deborah, Kasioka. Yes, all these children came from the poorest conditions and still had smiles on their faces.

When the orphans were singing praises to the Lord, the walls of the hall almost fell down like the ones of the town of Jericho, that fell after Joshua and his warriors had sung and played. I was deeply touched when I saw the children singing to the Lord with all their voices and hearts. I sometimes felt ashamed – we people in relatively rich parts of the world have everything and do not seem to give praise to Him like that. But here… orphans…children, mostly without parents, having experienced neglect, abuse, and lives we cannot even imagine, give God such praise despite all of that.

At the beginning of my ministry in the First Love Children's Home, I thought that I would mostly teach others and not learn very many new things. I was ready to give and not so much to receive, because I thought there was not much to receive…I was mistaken; I learned so much through my stay there that I can hardly name all of it. I not only gained training and experience in working with children, organizing events for their free time, teaching in the school, but also inspiration from the locals as to how to approach faith. Very friendly in public and private, Kenyans are unusually open in this respect. They are not ashamed that they are Christians. They ask you directly how you are with God and are ready to give you advice if you are in trouble. It made me smile when the headmaster proudly announced to me with great excitement when I was leaving the school, that he was an evangelist telling people about the Good News.

When you come to the Children's Home and see the children, you are ready to give them all you have. You give sacrificially to them so that you please their hearts, you love them and they love you, although they sometimes hurt you - be it through their behavior, or words whose meaning they may not fully realize. You see very soon that the children need our love. They may carry wounds from their early childhood when they were neglected or abandoned by their parents, when they starved or were misused. How many times did I tell myself when I felt hurt – "Have mercy! Mercy on the poor children!" And I received healing.

As a new volunteer or missionary, you will come to the place of your ministry and may have a naïve image that all will be ideal, the relationships with the locals and other people will be without problems, and that even the work with children will be relaxed and bring no major crisis. But there are crises. I made mistakes and stumbled. Sometimes I fell. A very kind nurse and friend, who worked in the Home, told me that it is sad but there may be conflicts where you would never expect them - even among missionaries. After all, they are people like anyone else and people are sinners and make mistakes. There were even cultural challenges and I sometimes failed at being sensitive and thoughtful enough.

How many times I reminded myself of Psalm 23, *"Even though I may walk through the valley of death, still you are with me,"* when I suffered from fever or when herds of large cows, flocks of goats, or roosters and camels walked towards me with their shepherd boy sometimes walking far behind.

"I admire you so much, I could not do it myself," I heard from some people around me. "Don't admire me, please. I would not have made it without...God; it is true," I said to them.

To live with him is great, but it is not possible to say that it is just about having fun and a good time always, 24/7. Of course, these are present in your life with him, but even harder times may come. God shapes us like a diamond. To make a diamond into a beautiful shiny stone it takes a lot of pressure, as a Kenyan pastor said one day. Some tension in your life may come from unforgiveness which, in many cases, you can do something about. And this was even my problem. I wanted to reconcile with my boyfriend who I caused suffering to. I knew I had God's forgiveness, but it was also important to settle things with him personally. What peace I experienced when I finally told him I was sorry, or when I met with Anna once, and we put things right … it was a good talk we had that day. I am also grateful for reconciliation with Lydia and her forgiveness. It's not only a lack of forgiveness that can cause pressure on you. It is also lies. But when you have told the truth to those around you, you are free.

In the end...not in vain, did John Huss write in his book (I will paraphrase), "That is why, faithful Christian, seek the truth, hear the truth, learn about the truth, love the truth, speak the truth, keep the truth, defend the truth until your death, because the truth will deliver you from sin, from the devil, from the death of your soul and finally from eternal death, which is eternal separation from God's grace" [Výklad viery 1412 / Interpretation of Faith 1412].

Huss is well known in the Czech Republic. "Don't ask me about Czech history, I know only when John Huss was burnt at the stake in 1415," a man said, when he was asked about some data from Czech history by a reporter on the street. Huss was a priest who strove for the restoration of the Church to follow Christ, rather than earthly principles.

And Huss was whom I got to talk about to a man on a train. He dashed into my compartment one late afternoon and hurriedly asked for permission to sit there. Without pausing he continued, "What are you reading?"

"Well...right now I am reading a book...about how to be a woman according to God's own heart." "Ouch ... that sounds like Jehovism." "I am not a Jehovah Witness, but yes, I am a Christian... What about you?" I think this question surprised him. "Well, I am on my way to become a Catholic." That is how our talk about faith started. Even though he did not believe, still this man wanted to be baptized.

The man mentioned Huss as a man not understood by his contemporaries and many after him, He recommended to me that I read a particular book revealing what his ministry was about. We talked about Czech history also.

I could not help crying as I read the book, *The Czech Wells*, in which the author, David Loula, describes what an awakening there was in the Czech nation for many generations until the battle of the White Mountain in 1620. Prior to this defeat, Czechs were known for their honesty and faithfulness to the one and true God. There was even a saying in the Silesian area north of our country, "Are you Czech that you are so honest?" The situation of faith in our country now, with the majority of citizens not professing God, is the result of difficult times of religious oppression in Czech history. It caused, by the way, that the sweet saying about Czechs being honest as a result of their transformation by Christ, is no longer valid.

The image of the Czech had changed. Instead of honesty, one will often meet with lack of loyalty, criticism, envy and other character traits left behind by it. "Our society is corrupt," he said, "can it change?" I explained that in order for us to be different, we need to acknowledge that we have done something wrong, and need to give and receive forgiveness and transformation from the Lord. A real change in society starts with you...

When we were saying goodbye, he was leaving me with a big smile on his face, saying, "The talk with you was like a pleasant shower." Is his baptism going to confirm his faith one day and is he going to become part of the change here which he wished for so much…?

We all long to be happy and we look for happiness in so many things. Many times the tiny and seemingly unimportant things, which we want, only point at what we need so much. Augustine was right when saying, "Restless is our heart until it comes to rest in you." In our hearts there will always be a little spot which we can try filling with many things, but still it will be unful-filled if the spot is not filled with God. He knows about your life, things you like, what makes you happy, but also your wounds and suffering, things you have done, the time you called upon his name, not even believing in him, asking him for help. If you come to him, he will not turn his back on you, just as he did not reject me either, and will receive you with joy.

This has been my journey to God and with God. I can believe in him, thanks to his grace and thanks to people he sent to me. Where would I be now if Dan had not come to our class before? But I am here the way I am, having received love, hope, peace, and support from him who is ready to give it to you, also. Let us not miss out on this opportunity, as an indi-vidual or as a nation. A person can testify about God in various ways, but the best is when you can have a first-hand experience of the wall coming down and a new relationship beginning. Are you ready to taste and see that the Lord is good?

Dear Lord,

Thank You for giving us this opportunity to come together through this book. Whether we have welcomed you to our hearts or not yet, may nobody remain unchanged by You. Jesus, You said, "Who comes to me I will never drive away." You are a good God. You do not favor anyone and long to give all people never ending life. In You there is all that every human heart is looking for. Thank You that You have a great plan for the life of each of us… Amen.

By Dan

"Dan, I'll finish most of my course work for my Master's Degree next spring. Before I write my thesis I wish to take a year to serve Jesus and others as a missionary somewhere. I'll need your help." Jane gave me that news Halloween weekend of 2012.

The news surprised me because I didn't expect it, yet it didn't astonish me since it was in keeping with her heart and character.

One of the observations that frequently amazes me is the wonderful way people can serve others and find pleasure in it. When you watch or read the news, you are presented with the depth and breadth of human depravity and its capacity to act inhumanely. The European castles and museums of the Middle Ages feature authentic torture chambers with implements I will not inflict on you via description. While the fifteenth and sixteenth centuries are famous for dungeons and the rack, it is the twentieth and twenty-first centuries that are notorious for massive genocides.

But it is the opposite that astounds me. I wonder how so many people can be so kind. Prague is considered by many tourists to be the most beautiful city in Europe. It is the one major capital city in Europe that escaped the devastation of bombardment in World War II. The medieval squares and castles of Prague are not restorations, but authentic originals often dating back to before Columbus' western hemispheric discoveries. That makes tourism an extra delight, but it also means Prague has more steps and fewer escalators than other cities. Often when coming up out of an underground metro, a young man has rescued Nancy and me by taking luggage from our hands and carrying it to the landing atop, setting it down, giving us a winsome smile before walking away pleased with himself. He relieved us of our burdens, but felt no burden in doing so. His soul found delight in serving us.

I witness such inner kindness daily. For every act of road rage, I experience dozens of driver courtesies; for every rude store clerk, I meet dozens eager to answer questions and help in any way possible. The opening paragraphs of the Bible tell us that the human race was created in the likeness of God. However far torture chambers and genocides have taken generations from that divine beginning, each act of kind service is a glimpse of God's original design, still shining through. The human race is now bi-polar, and within each of us resides, and often reveals, the worst of our fallen nature, yet also the beauty of the original model.

In the Czech Republic, when an atheist becomes a believer in God and Jesus Christ, several observations will confirm the change as real, as a new beginning, a spiritual birth, an awakened personality. Service is consistently one of these revelations. Parents are startled to observe lazy teens becoming diligent, chores being done before being reminded and without nagging, and an aura of courtesy, new respect, and helpfulness. Earlier you read how Jane asked forgiveness of her parents for how she had hurt them. In her early teen years, Jane found pleasure, or tried to find pleasure, in a selfish rebellion. After Christ entered her life, she found pleasure in honoring her parents. But I don't wish to exalt Jane; this is what normally happens and I hear stories about this from parents, and sometimes from students who are startled to find themselves living a new way of service without consciously planning it.

So at the end of October, 2012, Jane expressed a desire to give a year to serve others. And I did nothing, not one little thing to help her. I didn't know how to help her, and I even wondered if this would be a lasting plan or a dream to pass and not be mentioned again. Was God leading her in this or was this an infatuation with a missionary ideal?

Four weeks later, Thanksgiving weekend, Jane told me again, "Dan, please remember that I wish to give a year to serve as a missionary somewhere, and I'm not able to solve this by myself." The European Union has funded exchange programs so that university graduates from Finland or Poland may come to the Czech Republic, to serve in a kindergarten or an art school or a retirement home, while Czech graduates may go to another country to volunteer in a similar manner. Jane and I brainstormed a verbal plus and minus chart for this option, and resolved nothing. The European service project was an idea without passion for either of us.

I now knew that this mission longing was not fading away, but growing stronger within her. Service was how Jane worshipped her Savior. Romans 12.1 in the New Testament, confirms that service in the form of sacrificial living is received by the Lord as true and active worship. In John's Gospel, Jesus modeled this as he *"got up from the meal, took off his outer clothing, and wrapped a towel around his waist. After that, he poured water into a basin and began to wash his disciples' feet, drying them with the towel that was wrapped around him"* [John 13.5, NIV]. Being a Christian leader would not be modeled in a haughty right to rule, but in acts of continuous service to the needs of those God entrusted to their care.

We can express our worshipful celebration of our Savior and his salvation many ways. In the churches I've served in the USA, we were blessed with great musicians to lead the public Sunday worship meetings. We may express our reverent awe and joy in God's love through singing, reading, praying and giving. We also had those who found their pleasure in caring for little babies in the church nursery, and there were ushers with warm welcoming hearts who greeted people, learned their names and knew where they preferred to sit and escorted them to their seats. Occasionally someone would whisper to me, "I feel so sad for the helpers in the nursery and the ushers in the halls because they are seldom free to worship with us in the church's meetings." But I knew, that as with Jane, service was their spiritual gift of worship expression. They worshipped Jesus by changing diapers or in greeting people and helping them to a pew.

So Jane really wanted to serve somewhere...but where and how?

It was now Christmas season, and Jane told me the third time, "Dan, I feel God calling me to serve him and I can't arrange this alone. Please help me."

How could I remain inactive another day? I told her I'd write to some mission leaders and find options for her. Within days, we learned that one option was Honduras and I thought that would be exciting, educational, and full of worshipful service to people in their needs. Jane had recently been learning Spanish and would be able to communicate with Hondurans. The Philippines seemed a likely possibility for a brief time. A third option with an offer was the Children's Home of First Love International in Nairobi, Kenya.

Everything about the Kenyan opportunity stirred Jane's heart with enthusiasm. I didn't know that Africa was where she secretly wished to go. She didn't tell me because she didn't want to manipulate the process. She was willing to go where God would call her, and God was true to his Word, *"Take delight in the LORD, and he will give you the desires of your heart"* [Psalm 37.4, NIV].

Jane would go to Nairobi, Kenya, which was her dream destination, and the invitation wasn't manufactured by her, but was a gift from her God and Savior.

Almost immediately the gift turned into something that felt un-gift like. Jane must raise funds in order to go to Kenya for the 2013-2014 school year. Fund raising was nothing that had entered her mind and it was shocking.

Jane, her family, and many of our Czech friends logically argued, "When you are a volunteer, you don't have to pay. The organization you are volunteering to help, pays what is required." The European Union service program was offered as a prime example.

It was my role to explain that someone always pays. With the European volunteer service programs, it is the citizens of the countries who pay through taxes. African health projects may be funded by the Bill Gates Foundation or another foundation. In these cases, Bill Gates or wealthy donors pay for the volunteer workers. But Christian service missions are not funded by taxes and rarely by foundations fat with wealth. We must prayerfully seek God's provision, and we must let friends know of the need.

The fright of fundraising turned to the ecstasy of praise. Jane rarely needed to ask for funds...friends eagerly offered to give. Jane's mother met one of Jane's former teachers in a grocery store. The teacher inquired about Jane's life and plans, and mom told the teacher that Jane would go this autumn as a volunteer to a Children's Home in Kenya. The teacher's immediate response was, "This is wonderful. I want to help. How and where would I give to support this?" This set the tone for the next three months.

We learned that people would view this mission as important, and that they wanted to participate. It seemed no one wanted to be left behind. They wished to feel that they traveled with Jane and they would do it by giving; Christian believers would go with her by giving and praying also. The Litomyšl and Svitavy Církev bratrská churches sponsored a Czech version of an American garage or rummage sale. Hundreds of people donated items, crowds came to purchase, and the amount raised was above any expectation.

Spring is the time Nancy and I visit USA churches to tell about our past year and to raise funds to sponsor the summer English Camp. I wondered how I could manage fundraising for both the Kenya mission and English Camp. Far from being a problem, it will remain a highlight of memories for years to come. This was the spring when God's people came through and shined their very best. They gave eagerly, joyfully and generously, confirming the words of Jesus, *"It is more blessed to give than to receive"* [Acts 20.35, NIV].

One church seemed to be extra responsive as I explained the opportunity to partner with Jane for the Children's Home service in Kenya. After the morning worship service, Nancy and I went to the vestibule to greet people and a lady rushed up and said, "I'll never forget that wonderful morning when Jane came to visit our church." I knew that Jane had never been to this Wisconsin church and tried to politely explain this. The lady was undeterred...she remembered Jane and that special Sunday morning. Quickly others gathered to fill in the details. Eighteen months earlier, the pastor had played the YouTube video of Jane and the Svitavy English Camp group singing, "Oh Happy Day." The preacher had used this video to illustrate some part of his message. Eighty Sundays had come and gone since, but that three minute video had imprinted God's grace in their hearts in a way they could never forget. It seemed that Jane had actually been there. Many gave of their wealth, or gave from their poverty, to be on that plane when it flew to Kenya with Jane.

Dr. Tom Clinton, the Director of First Love International Ministries, wrote a description of what Jane's service would actually be.

Jane Vlčková Job Description:

Tutor our 80 boys and girls in the English language at our First Love Kenya Children's Home.

- Organize and Direct an English Reading and Writing club at our First Love Kenya Children's Home.
- Assist our children's home boys and girls with their homework assignments each day after school.

- Assist with cooking and cleaning chores at the children's home as needed.
- Assist in counseling and discipling girls at the children's home.
- Assist the First Love Kenya social worker and nurse with their responsibilities as needed.
- Provide care for the girls who live on your floor in the girls' dormitory during the evening hours as needed.
- Teach English to Kenyan boys and girls at schools which are a part of the First Love Association as the opportunity arises.

Jane arrived in Nairobi, Kenya in September of 2013, four days before Muslim terrorists from Somalia murdered many shoppers and workers while taking control of a Nairobi shopping mall. We were all alarmed for Kenya, for Jane, and I was especially alarmed for Jane's mom and dad. It's not easy to let go of a daughter...for a year...to Africa. They feared for her travel safety, for her water supply and health, for all the things that any parent would be concerned about. Yes, mom and dad were now praying Christian believers, who trusted in God's care and had given their parental blessing on this mission year, but that didn't eliminate all concerns. I prayed for all, the safety of the children in the orphanage, for Jane, and especially for peace in the hearts of her parents, sister and Grandma. The children and Jane were all safe and the orphanage was never threatened.

I arrived in Nairobi with Jane's sister, Eva, in February, mid-way through Jane's year of service. At the airport gate in Amsterdam minutes before departing, an African government official overheard our conversation about going to the children's home next to the Kibera slum. This slum has one million inhabitants in a 2 square mile area. The official interrupted to shake our hands, give us a polite shoulder hug, and to thank Eva and I for going to Kibera, for being with a mission organization that rescues the children in the largest slum in the entire African continent. The government of Kenya had welcomed us with open arms...literally.

That began my early impressions of Kenyans. They were warm, friendly, talkative and hospitable. At the Nairobi airport it seemed every employee was happy and greeted us with authentic, helpful intentions. That impression never changed. Kenya is a more Christian nation, and God's kindness can regularly be experienced there.

First Love Kenya, our children's home, impressed me beyond my expectation. It was safe, clean, professional, also full of love, yet with required order and discipline. The staff is not doing a duty; they are caring for these children as their own. The children attend Kenyan public schools and receive a normal education. They learn of God's love and experience it through those they call mom and dad on the staff. Even the gardeners have God's love for the children. Jane quickly learned the names of all 83 children and they soon adored her.

Jane visited a public school and was invited to be an English and art teacher. Eva and I visited this school and watched the children flock to Jane, running to her when they saw her. It reminded me of the concerns and worries people had for Jane before she left. They worried about her diet and water and health; they feared she would have culture shock and not be able to last the year; they had concerns for her acceptance and security as a Czech in Africa. And I remember my wife's single reservation. Nancy said, "Jane's only struggle will be that she will grow to love these children so much, it will be difficult for her to leave them at the end of the year." Of all the frets of Czech and American friends, Nancy's was the most on target.

Jane returned to Svitavy in late June, 2014, and three weeks later was a key leader in our English Camp. She taught African music, sang with the band, helped teach and translate English, and told her life story and testimony. Weeks before, she was doing all of these in Nairobi. Since camp, she has spent many days with girl campers, befriending and mentoring them as she did children in Kenya. She is writing her

Master's thesis and will go to university in Pilsen again, but she plans to return regularly to Svitavy to lead English Clubs and serve in every way she can.

This is our story, but behind it all, and through all, is the love and grace of God in Christ. It is his story; history is his story, God's story, especially with Jane.

This is our story, until now, but Jane's adventure in walking with Jesus is still young; new chapters are being written in her life daily. As I anticipate what may yet be, I think of the older British leader mentoring a young American. Early in the 19th century, Henry Varley challenged D. L. Moody: *"It remains to be seen what God will do with the man who is fully consecrated to him."* Moody became such a person, and he was privileged to speak as Christ's ambassador to 100 million people, before the age of radio, television and the internet. It remains to be seen what God will do with Jane, and many of her friends also mentioned in this book.

This is our story, but you can write your own story, if not on paper, then in flesh and spirit, in the hearts and memories of those who know you.

The story of your life, with God's grace and power in you, begins with a rebirth from who you are into the new man or woman infused with God's Spirit and power. Everyone's path back to the Father begins with repentance; that stirring in the heart that something is not right, and that what is not right is in me. Repentance is that 'aha' awakening that the problems that hinder, hold and even harm me, are not with governments, nor with schools, culture or friends. It is the recognition that my life is missing the target, daily falling short of what a man or woman should be, and I need God's strength to turn my life to a new direction, a healthy and holy path I now long for.

The story of your life with God's grace will be awed with the dawning awareness that God loves you, not because you are better or lesser than anyone else, but just because he loves you [Deuteronomy 7.7&8]. In God's love for you, he entered this world in the person of Jesus; we remember this event as Christmas. Jesus lived and served in a way that never missed the target God had for his life; always reached the goal, day by day. This was not easy, even for him. He lived through the resources of prayer, dependence on God's power and Spirit, and obeying God's Word. Every resource that enabled Jesus is available to you and me.

The story of your life will include that the One who never missed the mark, was nailed to the cross in place of us who consistently fall short of God's target, morally, socially, relationally, spiritually, publically and privately. Jesus took God's wrath against our sin so that we could be rescued and redeemed.

How beautiful is this to know and trust?! "When we were utterly helpless, Christ came at just the right time and died for us sinners. Now, most people would not be willing to die for an upright person, though someone might perhaps be willing to die for a person who is especially good. But God showed his great love for us by sending Christ to die for us while we were still sinners. And since we have been made right in God's sight by the blood of Christ, he will certainly save us from God's condemnation. For since our friendship with God was restored by the death of his Son while we were still his enemies, we will certainly be saved through the life of his Son. So now we can rejoice in our wonderful new relationship with God because our Lord Jesus Christ has made us friends of God" [Romans 5.6-11, NLT].

As slaves in ancient times could be bought and set free by someone who loved them and had the wealth to pay the price, so God redeems and frees us, through the payment that included Jesus' bloody death. The warranty and receipt stamped 'paid in full' is the resurrection of Jesus. Our Redeemer lives again.

The story of your life with God's grace will begin with prayer. *"If you openly declare that Jesus is Lord and believe in your heart that God raised him from the dead, you will be saved. For it is by believing in your heart that you are made right with God, and it is by openly declaring your faith that you are saved. As the Scriptures tell us, 'Anyone who trusts in him will never be disgraced.' Jew and Gentile are the same in this respect. They have the same Lord, who gives generously to all who call on him. For 'Everyone who calls on the name of the LORD will be saved'"* [Romans 10.9-13, NLT].

When you pray, acknowledging your sins, declaring Jesus as the Redeemer who paid the price, and affirming your trust in him, what will happen? At least 33 marvelous things will happen, including your new birth, your welcome in the family of God, and the beginning of your new story.

At camps and clubs and schools, both Jane and I are asked many questions about our stories. Who are you? What are your hobbies? What have you seen in your travels? Tell us about your family. Why do you volunteer your time to be with us and to help us? Why do you believe in God?

I enjoy answering such questions and my first three weeks each school term, in the five Czech high schools I teach in, are get-acquainted days. We play ice-breaker games and intentionally work to know each other. I tell students my journey from Kenosha, Wisconsin to Svitavy, The Czech Republic, and I'm not shy to tell them I'm there to share God's love and help them find their way back to God. I have more liberty to speak of my faith in the most atheistic nation in the world than any public school teacher in the USA, but I know there are boundaries to be respected. To answer a question is acceptable, but to preach a sermon in the school is to cross a line...or a wall.

To help answer some of these questions, Jane and I collaborated on a project. One of America's favorite Christian tracts or pamphlets is printed in Wheaton, Illinois by Good News Publishers. It is titled, "You're Special." We received permission to translate and print this in the Czech Republic, and this has been done. It is now popular nationwide.

But some want to know not just why a person might believe, but "Why, Dan, do YOU believe?" God bless you reader; I hope someday to hear the story God has written with your life. Now, here is one way I answer the personal "Why" question.

Why Do You Believe?

"To be or not to be?" Shakespeare's Hamlet asked.
I exist and you exist in some form...but what?
And when we cease to exist here, shall we exist
in another place and form and dimension?

For this current existence what does it mean "to be?"
Am I a material accident or do I have a soul?
Am I an evolutionary nothing, a brief incident,
a candle flame, or am I something divine?

"We hold these truths to be self-evident, that all
men are created equal, that they are endowed by
their Creator with certain unalienable Rights,"
entitled by "the Laws of Nature and of Nature's God."

Thomas Jefferson and his American revolutionary
friends wrote and signed their inner convictions

with ink on parchment; many more with blood on soil.
The American experiment is founded on our connection to God.

Men and women are intrinsically valuable,
precious, free and equal because
God made us that way. We exist for
God's purposes, by, and for his love.

Therefore man does not answer to government;
Both man and government answer to God;
and government is accountable to both God and man
who bears God's image. Self-evident they called it.

"Why do you believe in God?" the student inquired.
It is a just and fair question, and also a new one
in the history of humanity and nations.
What was once self-evident is now fogged over.

So why do I believe in God?
The foundation of my faith is rational,
although atheists claim the same starting point,
so it is reason and other reasonable elements.

I believe in God because there is no other
explanation for how things came to be.
"In the beginning God created" remains the
singular satisfactory account.

In 1960, scientists could be excused
for ignorantly suggesting life began
with a lightning strike in a scummy pond,
but there is no excuse in the 21st century.

Now we know that the smallest single cell
organisms have DNAs as complex as humans.
The miniature amoeba is immensely more complex
than science permits accidental probability.

Indeed, has there ever been a random genetic change
that produced an improvement in any creature?
Genetic changes are mutations resulting in deformities;
Darwin's new religion remains a speculation of blind faith.

I believe in God because I observe consciences guilty,
moral indignations at crime and injustice,
repugnance for corruption and slavery,
revealing God's universal moral law written in human hearts.

I believe in God because I observe and enjoy
kindness instead of devouring the weak,
laughter and humor that is so human it is divine,
and love...sacrificial love...showing God still in us.

I believe in God because my atheist grandma
killed herself by hanging, in the Great Depression.
My mother learned that atheism offers no hope
or reason why life should be treasured or endured.

My dad's family was raised in the kind of wealth
to inspire capitalist or communist jealousy.
But in the same Great Depression, the Luptons lost all,
and wealth proved to be a lying foundation to life.

My parents married and became believers,
living with faith experiences and answers to prayer.

I watched and measured and evaluated,
and then I concluded that they had found reality.

I believe in God because I find
the story of Christ's life fully credible.
Not one disciple believed in the resurrection
quickly, easily or willingly.

But when they believed, that faith carried them
in joy and in sorrow, in life and in death.
"To be" meant a spiritual birth, God's presence,
love for others, answered prayers, and the promise of Heaven.

The day I put my trust in God and Christ
I was a student in Jackson, Michigan.
God called me to come to him; wooed me in a way
that demanded my response. How would I answer?

I abandoned the arrogance that pushed him away…
Intuitively, I always knew he was there.
In humility, I came as a rebellious son
desiring to be forgiven and reconciled to "Dad."

That was fifty years ago…A lifetime,
not-yet-believers can't imagine how
real and personal and close God can be,
what it's like to converse with him.

Each day I watch for "God-sightings." Each evening
I celebrate the ways he's been with me,
little moments and big miracles, unique events,
all affirming that I'm invaluable to God.

I believe, because the Lord is my Shepherd,
guiding, protecting and providing for me.
God is now my Father, which is all God wants;
to have a loving Fatherly relationship with each of us.

I believe God is, and knows our names,
thinks about us, and loves each of us.
How one crosses from unbelief to knowing God is
a mystery, but when it happens, it's full of beauty and life.

 * *U.S.A. Declaration of Independence, July 4, 1776*

J. Daniel Lupton, 2010

Perspective, Historical and Current

Every drama, whether fiction or real life story like ours, cinematic or live theatre, requires a venue, featuring a set with scenery within a stage, studio or locale, which suggests the location and time period of the story. The locale is Svitavy, a town in the center of the Czech Republic, which is the center of Europe. Svitavy's most famous citizen was Oscar Schindler of the "Schindler's List" movie, produced/directed by Steven Spielberg and which starred Liam Neeson as Schindler. Those 1,200 Jewish lives were rescued in a nearby factory, and in the winter when the leaves are down, I can see the Schindler family home from our apartment window.

Our opening scene is in a Svitavy classroom and the time element is recent, almost current. But the story is connected to roots in communist socialism, two world wars, the American colonies and even medieval times. Our story is as local as a small town newspaper, and yet so global it spans three continents. You'll need to imagine your own musical score, while the camera pans over a historic backdrop, before we take a seat in a tense European school room.

The Czech Republic, formerly within Czechoslovakia, now encompasses the regions of Bohemia and Moravia. After suffering one party communist rule for forty years, the Czech Republic emerged to be the economic leader of the former USSR nations. It exports more than it imports, has a balanced national budget, and provides quality education through university, along with universal health care.

The enduring legacy of the communist era, however, also includes a reputation for corruption, along with weakened values regarding marriage, morality, and religious or spiritual faith. The Christian faith has been replaced with atheism, and Czechs frequently claim, with some pride, of being the world's most atheistic nation. Christians were persecuted for two recent generations and survival was the challenge for the churches permitted to exist during much of the second half of the 20th century.

It wasn't always this way. It was the Czech people who give us the Evangelical Protestant Reformation 100 years before Martin Luther, while also becoming the first nation to practice religious freedom and respectful toleration of other faith traditions through the Kutna Hora Declaration of 1485. During a two century enlightened era, the Czech people became the greatest spiritually alive and educationally literate culture in history, to that time.

This powerful period began with the voice and pen of John Huss (Jan Hus), the pillar-pastor-priest-educator who stood tall and loud for truth, independence, and a reformed Christian church where no leader or organization was above God, Biblical instruction and the conscience of an individual. For this he was martyred by burning at a stake, July 6, 1415. But what Rome and the Hapsburgs intended to destroy, grew until 90% of Bohemians and Moravians were praying, Biblically well-read, and broadly educated citizens. At this time there was an idiom that any farmer's wife could instruct a pastor since they all knew the Bible equally well. Six of the world's first ten printing presses were in the Czech lands to print educational materials for schools, and Bibles.

This epoch era concluded with a second pillar, the Bishop of the Unity of the Brethren and educator, John Amos Comenius [Czech: *Jan Amos Komensky*], who is considered universally as the father of modern education. Comenius led his Bohemians and Moravians to be the first in the world to educate equally boys and girls, peasants and children of the noble class. [Later, in exile, he organized school systems for Sweden and Holland, and was asked to be the President of Harvard University, which he declined].

The Hapsburgs could not tolerate this spiritual and educational movement because it would not bow and submit...it fostered a spirit of freedom, of accountability to God and conscience, rather than to kings and religious councils.

So, in 1620 the counter-reformation armies beheaded key evangelical and national Czech leaders and compelled everyone to return to the Church of Rome. The tipping day was November 8, 1620, with the Battle of White Mountain. The Hapsburg Holy Roman Empire conquered the Czech lands, ending 200 years of freedom with faith. It became illegal to own a Bible or attend a protestant church service. Soon the Czech population dwindled from 3 million to 800,000, as three quarters chose to flee into exile. Freedom and faith were more important to these than houses, farms and businesses.

Many fleeing persecution in Czech lands found refuge on Count Zinzendorf's German estate and built the community of Herrnhut. At Herrnhut they organized the greatest missionary movement in the history of the Christian church. Moravian Czech missionaries sold themselves into slavery in the West Indies to introduce slaves to Christ. They took the love of Jesus to India and Africa and Europe...and the American colonies.

While the Battle of White Mountain, November 8, 1620, ended two centuries of freedom of conscience and faith, the Pilgrims on the Mayflower were approaching the coast of the new world, sighting land the next day,

November 9, 1620. In the following days the Pilgrims and sailors wrote the Mayflower Compact, agreeing to democratic principles while honoring God. The baton for freedom, politically and religiously, passed from the Czech nation to the North American Continent.

America became a Christian nation, however, primarily through the Great Awakening of the 1740s, led by the British preachers George Whitfield and John Wesley. These two were influenced and discipled by Czech Moravians. Wesley's journal tells his story of meeting the Moravians and how he came to faith in Jesus through them. Whitfield's "last will" gave all his property to the Moravian Church in appreciation for their value in his life and their service to the world. The spiritual awakening in the colonies also generated a spirit of freedom, leading to the Declaration of Independence. One of the authors and signers of the U.S. Constitution was Richard Bassett, a Moravian in exile.

The USA, until recently, was a Christian nation. We trace America's faith history upstream to the Great Awakening in the colonies, to Czech exiles in Herrnhut, and ultimately to the head waters in Prague, Litomyšl and Kunvald, in the Czech Republic. This is the region of Jane Vlčková and where the Luptons have made their home for a decade. I've often told Czech people that I'm there to thank them for bringing freedom and Christ to my nation, and I wish to return the favor.

Today visitors to the Czech Republic often claim that Prague is the most beautiful city in all of Europe. It is certainly the most authentic, because Prague was not destroyed in WWII. Castles, dating to before Columbus, can be enjoyed alongside beautiful nature throughout the country. The people are ambitious educationally, advanced in technology and engineering, but prefer to live modestly materially. The Bohemian and Moravian tastes, steep this culture in art and music.

J. Daniel Lupton

Acknowledgements

Much of what I can do or have accomplished is thanks to my parents' great love, tolerance, support and environment. I thank them both for this. I thank my dear friends Dan and Nancy Lupton who did not hesitate and stepped out of their comfort zone to come to our country, and that they have always been here for us. I thank Dan for everything he has done for me, some of which is here – his advice, support, help, driving me home by car ☺, and being my mentor. I also thank our editors Pat Scott and Nela Prokešová and translator Míla Marková for their unflagging help and inspiring advice during the process of writing this book. I am grateful to Tino for his comments on the book. I thank God.

Jane

As with Jane, I'm thankful to my devoted parents. I miss their mentoring encouragement...they always believed in me and helped light my path. I'm grateful to Nancy, my faithful wife and friend for nearly five decades, and the first listener and counselor with my every idea. I thank, and miss, Charles Svoboda, my Czech/American mentor for 40 years, who welcomed every request for time to hear my stories and questions. I'm humbly grateful to American friends from every chapter of my life, from my teen years to now, who remain on my support team in a variety of ways; for Gary Page and the Carney English Camp Team, who have lived every chapter of this book with Jane and me. I'm in awe of my devoted Czech friends, school teachers and administrators who welcome me, and the Svitavy team who arrange everything from translation to auto repair... without them this book would not be. You needed the editing help of my friend Pat Scott to read this in English, and the translation of Míla Marková to read in Czech. Thank you both. I thank Jane's parents and sister Eva for their blessing, and I'm grateful for Jane. This is her story, with my commentary. I thank God for our amazing journey.

Dan

We thank two for their professional skills as this book neared completion. Jana Macková for Cover Photography. Dita Targoszová for Cover Design. You both served us perfectly.

Links and Contacts

Thanks for reading "*Meant to Be?*"

To see photos of Jane Vlčková, Daniel Lupton and some of the scenes mentioned in the book, please go www.meant.yolasite.com

To learn about the city Svitavy in the Czech Republic, go to www.svitavy.cz
   [To view in English, click the British flag on the home page.]

The Oscar Schindler exhibit in the Svitavy museum will be found at www. muzeum.svitavy.cz/
   [To view in English, click the British flag on the home page.]

If you have any comments, questions or a desire to contact the authors, you may write to Jane Vlčková or Daniel Lupton directly at: taste.meant@ gmail.com

Meant to Be? will soon be published in the Czech Republic in the Czech language. When we have the release date with Czech title and where you may purchase it, we will post it here: www.meant.yolasite.com